Environmental A

Government Departments

LONDON: HMSO

ISBN 0 11 752915 X

Foreword by the Minister for the Environment and Countryside

In the Strategy for Sustainable Development which we published in January this year, we promised further guidance on environmental appraisal to follow up the guide on "Policy Appraisal and the Environment" we published in 1991. This booklet looks at how government departments have used and applied the techniques described in that guide, and gives details of some specific studies.

Many of the studies described have been carried out under contract by private sector consultants and university departments. In some cases, the final policy decisions have yet to be taken. In others, the appraisals themselves are not yet complete. It would be wrong to pretend that the principles set out in "Policy Appraisal and the Environment" are being applied in every case as systematically and consistently as ideally we should like. Nevertheless, we think it is important to be open about what we are doing and to share the lessons we are learning.

A good start has been made, and the practical utility of good environmental analysis is clear enough. For example, recent research on two Environmentally Sensitive Areas shows that they provide excellent value for money.

We have found a number of the studies referred to here directly useful in our work on economic instruments, and you can trace their influence in the booklet we published in November 1993, entitled *"Making Markets Work for the Environment"*.

A process of cultural change is now under way which we hope will encourage policy makers in all areas of government to think about the environment in taking their decisions. I hope this booklet will contribute to that process.

June 1994

Contents

		Page
Summary		vii–viii
Chapter 1	**Introduction**	1
	References	7–8
Chapter 2	**Approaches to Environmental Appraisal in Government Departments**	9
	General guidance on environmental appraisal	9
	Business, the consumer and the environment	10
	Integrated Pollution Control	10
	Environmental valuation	11
	Overseas development	12
	References	13
Chapter 3	**The Application of Enviornmental Appraisal**	14
	Agriculture	16
	Forestry	18
	Land use planning: development plans	19
	Land use planning: projects	20
	Transport	21
	Channel Tunnel Rail Link	22
	Transport policy alternatives	25
	a) A470 Corridor Study	25
	b) Public transport options for the environment	26
	Water	27
	Flood and coastal defence; sea level rise	28
	Climate change	29
	Hazardous chemicals	30
	Waste management	32
	References	34–36

		Page
Chapter 4	**Environmental Evaluation Studies**	37
	Introduction	37
	The social costs of fuel cycles	38
	Stated preference scoping study	38
	The value of biodiversity in UK forests	39
	Forest recreation and amenity	40
	Environmentally Sensitive Areas (ESAs)	42
	Landfill and incineration	44
	Health and environment: radon	45
	References	46
Chapter 5	**Economic Instruments**	47
	Introduction	47
	Water quality	47
	Air quality	48
	Climate change	49
	a) Costs of policy options and international competitiveness	50
	b) Long term strategy on road fuel duties	51
	c) Tradeable credits to improve new car fuel economy	53
	Waste management and recycling	55
	The law of liability	57
	References	60
GLOSSARY		61

Summary

This booklet follows up the Department of the Environment's earlier publication "Policy Appraisal and the Environment: A Guide for Government Departments". That Guide helped policy makers understand why they needed to carry out environmental appraisals; this new booklet tries to show how some of them put the advice into practice.

Its publication was foreshadowed in the Second Year Report on the 1990 Environment White Paper, "This Common Inheritance", and in the "UK Sustainable Development Strategy" published in January 1994.

Chapter I offers a quick outline of some of the basic concepts of environmental appraisal, and points out some of the limitations. Chapter II reviews the advice available to Government Departments. Chapter III looks at appraisal techniques in practice through a series of examples in different policy areas. Chapter IV examines some of the particular problems associated with using monetary values in environmental appraisals, and illustrates some attempts to tackle the problems. Chapter V discusses ways of appraising the likely effectiveness of economic instruments, and this is a useful supplement to the Department's recent booklet "Making Markets Work for the Environment".

There are a number of different reasons why it may be desirable to embark upon environmental appraisal. First, it may be useful to undertake a systematic analysis of the environmental costs and benefits associated with a particular policy initiative; the cost-benefit analysis of the National Forest is an example. Second, studies may be needed to explore the wider economic implications of environmental policies such as greenhouse gas control strategies. Third, there are studies of the environmental implications of economic policies; an example is the development of the Land Use Allocation Model designed to explore

the environmental implications of the Common Agricultural Policy.
Fourth, there are studies designed to determine the cost-effectiveness
of alternative methods of delivering environmental policy objectives
such as targets for reducing emissions of acid gases. Fifth, there are
studies designed to explore how environmental externalities, such as
those arising from landfill and incineration, can be internalised. Finally,
there are studies designed to improve procedures for appraising costs
and benefits in particular policy areas, such as the control of hazardous
chemicals.

This booklet contains brief summaries of all these studies and many
more besides. The studies chosen are designed to be a representative
cross section of the work that is being done by and for government
departments. The examples chosen cover the three environmental
media - air, land and water - and the principal industries - agriculture,
construction, energy, manufacturing, and transport - which affect the
environment.

Chapter 1: Introduction

1.1   In 1991, the Department of the Environment published guidance under the title "Policy Appraisal and the Environment: A Guide for Government Departments".[1] This followed a review of the ways in which the environmental costs and benefits of policies are assessed within government departments. The review had concluded that there was scope for a more systematic approach within government.

1.2   A subsequent assessment found that the publication of "Policy Appraisal and the Environment" had made people aware of the need to appraise environmental costs and benefits systematically. This booklet tries to show how people have acted on that new awareness.

1.3   The basic principles of policy appraisal are easily stated. The Treasury guidance on general economic appraisal puts it well:

> **"Systematic appraisal entails being clear about objectives, thinking about alternative ways of meeting them, and estimating and presenting the costs and benefits of each potentially worthwhile option. Used properly, appraisal leads to better decisions by policy makers and managers. It encourages both groups to question and justify what they do. It provides a framework for rational thought about the use of limited resources."** [2]

1.4   Good policy decisions depend on the effective analysis of alternative options. A systematic appraisal ensures that the objectives of a policy are clearly laid out, and that the trade-offs between options are accurately identified and assessed. Appraisal is the process of identifying, quantifying and weighing up the costs and benefits of the measures which are proposed to implement a policy. All the implications of the options must be analysed, not just the financial ones.

---

[1] Department of the Environment (1991), *Policy Appraisal and the Environment: A Guide for Government Departments,* HMSO.

[2] HM Treasury (1991), *Economic Appraisal in Central Government: A Technical Guide for Government Departments* (para 1.2), HMSO.

1.5   The purpose of environmental appraisal is to ensure that environmental impacts are not ignored, and to make sure that they are integrated into the general appraisal of policy in a systematic way.

1.6   Appraisal is different from evaluation. Appraisal is an analysis of the likely implications of a decision before it is taken. Evaluation is an analysis of the effects of a decision after it has been taken and the consequences have had time to work themselves out. The way in which appraisal and evaluation should be used to help in the definition and refinement of policy objectives and options is illustrated in the flow diagram.

1.7   Although appraisal and evaluation happen at different times, they both use the same analytical framework, notably cost-benefit analysis. This booklet is not the place to describe cost-benefit analysis in detail. The interested reader will find more on the subject in the Treasury's "Green Book"[1] and in "Policy Appraisal and the Environment". In environmental appraisal and evaluation, environmental assessment (EA) will often be the means through which physical environmental impacts are addressed.

1.8   Financial appraisal of the kind carried out by investment analysts for private sector companies is concerned primarily with the profit and loss account. Costs and revenues are forecast carefully to determine whether a particular investment decision can be justified or not. Cost-benefit analysis is concerned with somewhat similar questions, but the difference is that the questions are asked from the point of view of society at large.

1.9   In cost-benefit analysis, as many impacts as possible are expressed in terms of the monetary value which society places on them; and the net benefit is derived as the basis for policy choices. A discount rate helps to compare costs and benefits which arise at different times.

1.10   An important aspect of cost-benefit analysis is the identification, quantification and valuation of costs and benefits which are not normally reflected in market prices. Environmental externalities often fall into this category. Techniques of environmental assessment have an important role to play in the physical measurement of environmental impacts. The techniques of monetary valuation which can be used to measure their importance are described in Appendix C of "Policy Appraisal and the Environment".

---

[1] HM Treasury (1991), *Economic Appraisal in Central Government: A Technical Guide for Government Departments* (para 1.2), HMSO.

The Process of Policy Appraisal

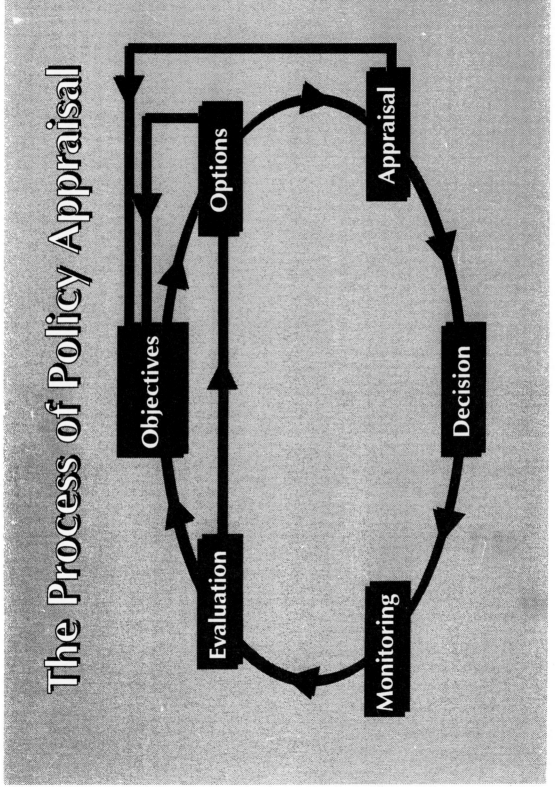

1.11   Almost every decision which affects the environment will entail costs. For example, a decision to reduce emissions of a pollutant will almost certainly produce costs, which can only be justified if the environmental benefits exceed these costs. The problem becomes one of how to quantify those environmental benefits. Money is usually the most convenient measuring rod for this purpose.

1.12   The criterion which is most widely used in cost-benefit analysis for determining whether or not benefits outweigh costs is the "Hicks-Kaldor" or the "potential Pareto" criterion. This criterion is satisfied if the gainers following any particular economic decision can, in principle, compensate those who lose, and still be better off than before. (This is regardless of whether compensation is actually paid.)

1.13   A particular challenge for environmental policy is to take account of the concept of sustainable development. This concept came to prominence with the publication, in 1987, of "Our Common Future: Report of the World Commission on Environment and Development", popularly known as the Brundtland Report.[1] The Brundtland Report defined sustainable development as:

> **"development that meets the needs of the present without compromising the ability of future generations to meet their own needs".**

1.14   The analytical implications of this concept have been much debated. In 1988 the Department of the Environment commissioned the London Environmental Economics Centre (LEEC) to examine the question, and their report, popularly known as the Pearce Report, was published the following year under the title "Blueprint for a Green Economy".[2] Professor Pearce and his colleagues have subsequently, on their own initiative, published two sequels: Blueprint 2[3] and Blueprint 3[4] which deal respectively with global environmental issues and the problems of measuring sustainable development.

1.15   Although there continue to be differences of view about what the concept of sustainable development means in practice, it seems reasonable to infer two things from it. First, we need to take proper account of the environmental consequences of what we do. Second, we have to take a view about the balance of both the man made wealth and natural capital that we should bequeath to future generations.

---

[1] Brundtland (1987), *Our Common Future: Report of the World Commission on Environment and Development*, Oxford University Press.

[2] D W Pearce, A Markandya and E B Barbier (1989) *Blueprint for a Green Economy*, Earthscan.

[3] D W Pearce et al (1991), *Blueprint 2, Greening the World Economy*, Earthscan.

[4] D W Pearce et al (1993), *Blueprint 3, Measuring Sustainable Development*, Earthscan.

1.16   This idea of balancing natural and man-made wealth to hand on to future generations has implications for environmental accounting and for risk assessment. The interested reader may wish to refer to the article on environmental accounting in the November 1992 edition of "Economic Trends",[1] or to the Report of a Royal Society study group on risk analysis,[2] to the Department of the Environment's paper on environmental risk assessment and management,[3] and the Department of Trade and Industry's 1993 booklet on risk assessment in relation to regulation making.[4]

1.17   The focus of this booklet is the UK environment but British economists have made significant contributions to international environmental appraisal efforts. For example, two volumes commissioned by the Overseas Development Administration (ODA) - the "Manual of Environmental Appraisal"[5] and "Values for the Environment"[6] were designed to help developing country economists as well as economists working for the ODA.

1.18   International organisations have a key role to play in the search for international consensus and consistent methodologies. The Organisation for Economic Cooperation and Development (OECD) has published "Environmental Policy Benefits: Monetary Valuation"[7] and is preparing its own manual of environmental appraisal.[8] The World Bank has published a technical paper entitled "Guidelines for Environmental Assessment of Energy and Industry Projects".[9]

1.19   A number of factors affect how far and how fast the findings of environmental appraisal will affect policy. It is important to remember that the purpose of environmental appraisal is to provide information; it is not a substitute for good judgement. Good appraisal can reduce the extent of the uncertainty confronting decision makers and it can inform public debate; it cannot make decisions.

---

[1] C Bryant and P Cook, *'Environmental Issues and the National Accounts',* Economic Trends No.469, November 1992, Central Statistical Office, HMSO.

[2] The Royal Society (1992), *'Risk: Analysis, Perception and Management',* Report of a Royal Society Study Group, London.

[3] Department of the Environment (forthcoming), *Risk Assessment and Risk Management for Sustainable Development,* HMSO.

[4] Department of Trade and Industry (1993), *Regulation in the Balance - A Guide to Risk Assessment,* HMSO.

[5] Overseas Development Administration (1992), *Manual of Environmental Appraisal,* HMSO.

[6] J Winpenny (1991), *Values for the Environment: A Guide to Economic Appraisal,* HMSO.

[7] D W Pearce and A Markandya (1989), *Environmental Policy Benefits: Monetary Valuation,* OECD.

[8] D W Pearce, D Whittington and S Georgiou (1994), *Project and Policy Appraisal: Integrating Economics and Environment,* OECD, Paris.

[9] World Bank (1991), *Environmental Assessment Source Book, Volume III, Guidelines for Environmental Assessment of Energy and Industry Projects, Technical Paper 154,* World Bank.

1.20　The next chapter of this booklet discusses the approaches to environmental appraisal used in government departments. Chapter III discusses how the principles set out in "Policy Appraisal and the Environment" are being applied to specific policy areas. Chapter IV refers specifically to environmental valuation studies whilst Chapter V describes case studies which address the design of economic instruments as an efficient means of implementing environmental policy.

1.21　Many of the case studies referred to in this booklet have been published and are therefore already in the public domain. Further information about the others can be obtained on request from:

Department of the Environment
Environmental Protection Economics Division
Room AG01
Romney House
43, Marsham Street
LONDON SW1P 3PY

References

Brundtland (1987), *Our Common Future: Report of the World Commission on Environment and Development*, Oxford University Press.

C Bryant and P Cook, *"Environmental Issues and the National Accounts"*, Economic Trends, No.469, November 1992, Central Statistical Office, HMSO.

Department of the Environment (1991), *Policy Appraisal and the Environment: A guide for government departments,* HMSO.

Department of the Environment (forthcoming), *Risk Assessment and Risk Management for Sustainable Development*, HMSO.

Department of Trade and Industry (1993), *Regulation in the Balance - A Guide to Risk Assessment*, HMSO.

HM Treasury (1991), *Economic Appraisal in Central Government: A Technical Guide for Government Departments*, HMSO.

Overseas Development Administration (1992), *Manual of Environmental Appraisal*, HMSO.

D W Pearce, A Markandya and E B Barbier (1989), *Blueprint for a Green Economy*, Earthscan.

D W Pearce et al (1991), *Blueprint 2, Greening the World Economy,* Earthscan.

D W Pearce et al (1993) *Blueprint 3, Measuring Sustainable Development,* Earthscan.

D W Pearce and A Markandya (1989), *Environmental Policy Benefits: Monetary Valuation*, OECD.

D W Pearce, D Whittington and S Georgiou (1994), *Project and Policy Appraisal: Integrating Economics and Environment*, OECD, Paris.

The Royal Society (1992), *Risk: Analysis, Perception and Management*, Report of a Royal Society Study Group, London.

J Winpenny (1991), *Values for the Environment: A Guide to Economic Appraisal*, HMSO.

World Bank (1991), *Environmental Assessment Source Book, Volume III, Guidelines for Environmental Assessment of Energy and Industry Projects, Technical Paper 154*, World Bank.

Chapter 2: Approaches to Environmental Appraisal in Government Departments

2.1 When "Policy Appraisal and the Environment" was published in 1991, the main purpose was to help departments to ensure that their policy decisions take environmental effects fully into account.

2.2 Up to 1991, most policy and project appraisals had consisted of a financial or economic assessment and a largely separate environmental assessment. These had only been brought together in a qualitative manner in forming the overall judgement. More systematic analytical frameworks had been little used. Subsequent monitoring has suggested that:

(i) departments still need more guidance on valuation techniques; and

(ii) there is still scope for the dissemination of best practice and for sharing experience. This would give departments the chance to compare studies against a wider range of earlier ones, and thus give policy makers more confidence in using (or discarding) their results.

2.3 The remainder of this chapter provides a brief summary of general guidance on environmental appraisal. Case study material and guidance on the application of environmental appraisal to particular areas of government policy is the subject of the next three chapters.

General guidance on environmental appraisal

2.4 The most important document on economic appraisal in government is the Treasury's "Green Book".[1] The first "Green Book" was published 25 years ago; the latest edition was published in 1991. Although it includes guidance on the analysis of impacts that do not involve market transactions (including environmental impacts), the importance of the "Green Book" lies in the common methodology for economic appraisal that it sets out for use in all government departments.

---

[1] ibid.

2.5   The publication in 1991 of "Policy Appraisal and the Environment" extended the advice on the environment contained in the "Green Book". Its purpose was to ensure that environmental effects are fully considered during policy appraisal. This advice applies across the whole range of government policies and programmes, and not just to those with direct environmental objectives. It is consistent with the guidance contained in the "Green Book".

Business, the consumer and the environment

2.6   When appraising policy proposals, government departments are required to prepare a compliance cost assessment (CCA). Its purpose is to inform ministers and officials of the likely costs to business of complying with new or amended regulations so that compliance costs can be assessed, and unnecessary burdens to business identified, well before a decision is taken on whether or not to introduce them. Guidance on how to prepare a CCA was published by the Department of Trade and Industry in 1992.[1] Although the guidance does not explicitly address environmental appraisal, it is appropriate to refer to it here to emphasise that, in devising frameworks of regulation for environmental protection purposes, it is necessary to have regard to the costs as well as the benefits of such regulation.

2.7   Compared to direct regulation, economic instruments are usually more cost-effective because they allow business and consumers greater flexibility in deciding exactly how they achieve environmental objectives. They also encourage innovation; they generate information; and they may contribute additional public revenue. The Department of the Environment has therefore published a booklet to draw these advantages to the attention of policy makers. "Making Markets Work for the Environment"[2] does not, however, assume that an economic instrument is always the right answer. In some cases direct regulation, or a mixture of direct regulation and economic instruments, may be appropriate in order to achieve environmental objectives.

Integrated Pollution Control

2.8   Her Majesty's Inspectorate of Pollution (HMIP) enforces Integrated Pollution Control (IPC) in England and Wales, by means of authorisations controlling the use of prescribed processes and substances in industries with the most serious potential to pollute. In Scotland, IPC is enforced by Her Majesty's Industrial Pollution Inspectorate and the local river purification authorities. IPC covers the three environmental media of air, water and land, and seeks to identify and enforce the best practicable environmental option (BPEO) across all media. The Environmental Protection Act 1990 requires

---

[1] Department of Trade and Industry (1992), *Checking the Cost to Business: A Guide to Compliance Cost Assessment,* DTI.

[2] Department of the Environment (1993), *Making Markets Work for the Environment,* HMSO.

the inspectorates to use authorisations to secure the use of best available techniques not entailing excessive cost (BATNEEC). The analytical framework currently used by HMIP for discharging their responsibilities was discussed at a seminar held in 1993 and is published in the consultation document entitled "Environmental, Economic and BPEO Assessment Principles for Integrated Pollution Control".[1]

Environmental valuation

2.9 The Scottish Office Industry Department and Scottish Enterprise commissioned a review of the concept of economic value as it applies to the environment, in particular in relation to the activities of these organisations.[2] In the first of two reports, consultants described five valuation methods: contingent valuation, contingent ranking, the travel cost technique, hedonic pricing, and the avoided cost approach. The report considered the relative merits of the valuation methods discussed, how they might be used in practice, and how easily they can be incorporated within overall investment appraisal schemes.

2.10 The second report tested two of these methods - contingent valuation and travel cost. It indicated that the methods work best when the environmental change under consideration is distinct and clearly understood by the affected population. It also indicated that the valuation methods offer a suitable way of valuing environmental change, but that due care and attention is needed in their application. The project, the survey methods, and the bid mechanism used need to be chosen carefully, particularly until confidence and skills amongst practitioners are established.

2.11 In the litigation arising from the grounding of the tanker Exxon Valdez in March 1989, Exxon was sued for pollution damages partly on the basis of an application of the contingent valuation method. The US National Oceanic and Atmospheric Administration (NOAA) commissioned a panel of specialists to report on the conclusions and the methods used. The relevance of the NOAA Panel report[3] to the UK project and policy appraisal context, and the wider implications of the report, have been discussed at a two day conference entitled "Environmental Valuation in Context" at St. Aidan's College, Durham on 24th - 25th March 1994. The Department of the Environment intend to publish a report of the conference proceedings.[4]

---

[1] Her Majesty's Inspectorate of Pollution (1994), *Environmental, Economic and BPEO Assessment Principles for Integrated Pollution Control: Consultation Document,* HMIP.

[2] N Hanley in association with ECOTEC Ltd, *The Valuation of Environmental Effects, Stages I and II.* Final reports published by the Scottish Office Industry Department/Scottish Enterprise as *ESU Research Papers No.22* (1990) and *No.27* (1992).

[3] K Arrow, R Solow, P Portney, E Leamer, R Radner, and H Schuman (1993), *Report of the NOAA Panel on Contingent Valuation,* Resources for the Future, Washington DC.

[4] Department of the Environment (forthcoming), *Environmental Valuation in Context: Proceedings of a Conference held on 24-25 March 1994 at St. Aidan's College, Durham.*

Overseas development

2.12   The Overseas Development Administration's (ODA) "Manual of Environmental Appraisal"[1] sets out basic principles and specifies that all proposals for new overseas aid projects should address environmental issues. Environmental factors should be taken into account from the earliest stage of a project and followed through at all subsequent stages - from design to evaluation. This involves a multi-disciplinary approach to environmental factors which addresses economic, social and technical issues. The manual was produced by ODA in 1989 and updated in 1992. It has been made widely available to other multilateral and bilateral aid agencies as well as to recipient governments.

2.13   ODA staff are required to ensure that aid-funded policies and programmes in which they are involved are environmentally sound. Where environmental standards have been set by developing countries they are regarded as a minimum requirement for ODA financed projects. Where there is no local legislation, advice is taken on appropriate standards. In particular, the World Bank's "Environmental Guidelines"[1] provide a useful source of information on recommended standards for a range of industries and major pollutants.

2.14   The Overseas Development Institute was commissioned by ODA to produce a companion to the "Manual of Environmental Appraisal". The result - "Values for the Environment: A Guide to Economic Appraisal"[1] - aims to give economists working in developing countries a single volume which summarises the state of the art on the methodology and practice of the economic appraisal of environmental effects. It also provides a wide range of case studies. ODA economists take full account of the principles set out in the guide in their work and ODA require consultants working for them to use it similarly. It is also designed to be helpful to developing country economists. "Values for the Environment" was published in 1991. A companion volume of case studies is in preparation.

---

[1] ibid.

References

K Arrow, R Solow, P Portney, E Leamer, R Radner, and H Schuman (1993), *Report of the NOAA Panel on Contingent Valuation*, Resources for the Future, Washington DC.

Department of the Environment (1993), *Making Markets Work for the Environment*, HMSO.

Department of the Environment (forthcoming), *Environmental Valuation in Context: Proceedings of a Conference held on 24-25 March 1994 at St. Aidan's College, Durham*.

Department of Trade and Industry (1992), *Checking the Cost to Business: A Guide to Compliance Cost Assessment*, DTI.

Her Majesty's Inspectorate of Pollution (1994), *Environmental, Economic and BPEO Assessment Principles for Integrated Pollution Control: Consultation Document*, HMIP.

N Hanley in association with ECOTEC Ltd, *The Valuation of Environmental Effects, Stages I and II*. Final reports published by the Scottish Office Industry Department/ Scottish Enterprise as *ESU Research Papers No. 22* (1990) and *No.27* (1992).

Chapter 3: The Application of Environmental Appraisal

3.1   The Second Year Report on the Environment White Paper[1] includes a commitment (Ref No 48) to build up a body of case study material on particular applications of the methods set out in "Policy Appraisal and the Environment" and to publish further guidance. The need for further general guidance has been discussed in the previous chapter. This chapter and the next two discuss how the guidance on the application of the principles set out in "Policy Appraisal and the Environment" is being met in selected areas of policy.

3.2   The UK Sustainable Development Strategy[2] indicates that government departments have to address a wide range of environmental policy considerations and the variety of environmental impacts with which they are concerned is correspondingly wide. Historically, the motivation for much of the early environmental legislation was concern for the protection of human health. This remains an important priority and is reflected, for example, in the research on hazardous chemicals and radon referred to in paragraphs 3.76-3.83[3] and paragraphs 4.38 - 4.41 respectively.[4]

3.3   A second concern is to conserve those natural resources which have an economic value and which are in finite, or potentially finite, supply. Concerns of this kind are addressed in research on flood and coastal defence, and on waste management and recycling discussed in paragraphs 3.65 - 3.72[5] [6] and paragraphs 3.84 - 3.90[7] respectively.

[1] Department of the Environment (1992), *This Common Inheritance: The Second Year Report,* HMSO.
[2] HM Government (1994), *Sustainable Development: The UK Strategy,* HMSO.
[3] Risk and Policy Analysts in association with Acer Environmental (1992), *Risk-Benefit Analysis of Hazardous Chemicals,* Report for the Department of the Environment.
[4] K Field, B Shoderu and C Normand (1993), *Cost Effectiveness of Measures to Reduce Radon in Existing Dwellings,* Report for the Department of the Environment.
[5] E C Penning-Rowsell, C H Green, P M Thompson, A M Coker, S M Tunstall, C Richards and D J Parker (1992), *The Economics of Coastal Management: A Manual of Benefit Assessment Techniques,* Belhaven Press.
[6] University of East Anglia (1991), *Economic Appraisal of Climate Induced Sea Level Rise: A Case Study of East Anglia,* UEA
[7] David Perchard Associates and KPMG Management Consultants (1992), *EC Directive on Packaging and Packaging Waste, Compliance Cost Assessment,* Report for the Department of Trade and Industry.

3.4   A third concern identified by the UK Sustainable Development Strategy is that people value aspects of the environment for their own sake and wish, so far as possible, to pass them on to future generations. This kind of concern is reflected in the development of the countryside impacts table and the Land Use Allocation Model (see below paragraphs 3.14 - 3.20) and the evaluation of Environmentally Sensitive Areas (ESAs) (paragraphs 4.27 - 4.33).

3.5   The final category of environmental concerns are to do with global issues, including in particular, climate change. This subject is the focus of research studies referred to in paragraphs 3.68 - 3.72[1] and paragraphs 5.13 - 5.31[2] below.

3.6   There are a number of different reasons for undertaking environmental appraisal. In some cases, the emphasis is on a systematic analysis of the costs and benefits associated with a particular policy initiative. An example is the cost-benefit analysis of the National Forest,[3] the justification for which is largely in terms of the landscape and recreational benefits.

3.7   In other cases, studies are designed to explore the economic implications of environmental policies. The study of the impact of greenhouse gas control strategies on UK competitiveness (paragraphs 5.14 - 5.18) and the related study of links between environmental and international trade policies (paragraphs 3.73 - 3.75) are examples of this kind.

3.8   Then there are studies of the environmental implications of economic policies. The development of the Land Use Allocation Model for example has been designed to explore the environmental implications of the Common Agricultural Policy.[4]

3.9   Again, there are studies to compare the relative cost-effectiveness of different means of delivering environmental policies. The studies of public transport options for the environment[5] and of the potential role of market mechanisms in the control of acid rain[6] are examples.

---

[1] National Economic Research Associates (1991), *Links Between Environmental and International Trade Policies.*

[2] J Pezzey (1991), *Impacts of Greenhouse Gas Control Strategies on UK Competitiveness,* HMSO.

[3] London Economics (1993), *National Forest Cost Benefit Analysis,* unpublished report for the Countryside Commission.

[4] See below paras 3.18-3.20.

[5] See below paras 3.54-3.60.

[6] London Economics (1992), *The Potential Role of Market Mechanisms in the Control of Acid Rain*, HMSO.

3.10   There are also studies of how environmental externalities can be internalised. An example of this kind of study is the recent work on the externalities of landfill and incineration.[1]

3.11   Finally, there are studies of how to improve procedures for appraising costs and benefits in particular policy areas. Examples are the risk-benefit analysis of hazardous chemicals[2] and the evaluation of environmental information for planning projects.[3]

3.12   Many of the case studies referred to in this booklet have been carried out by economists in consultancy firms and universities under contract to government departments. The studies aim to show a representative cross-section of appraisals involving environmental costs and benefits. The range of examples covers the three environmental media - air, land and water - and the principal industries - agriculture, construction, energy, manufacturing, transport - which affect the environment.

3.13   For convenience, work on environmental valuation and with economic instruments is discussed in Chapters IV and V respectively. Other appraisal studies are discussed in this chapter.

Agriculture

3.14   Two recent projects have looked at the impact of agriculture on the environment. These cover the construction of a countryside impacts table and a land use model.

3.15   One methodology of environmental policy appraisal, described in "Policy Appraisal and the Environment", uses an 'impacts table' or matrix of information. The axes of the matrix are the 'actions' which characterise a proposal and a set of 'environmental receptors' which are potentially affected by it. Entries in the cells of the matrix flag any environmental costs or benefits, or show whether the effects are neutral or unknown.

3.16   This methodology was used in a project the Department of the Environment commissioned from a team led by Roy Haines-Young at Nottingham University.[4] They constructed a countryside impacts table using a computerised database which can display the mechanisms linking actions to environmental receptors.

---

[1] CSERGE, Warren Spring Laboratory and EFTEC (1993), *Externalities of Landfill and Incineration*, Report to the Department of the Environment, HMSO.
[2] See below paras 3.76-3.83.
[3] See below paras. 3.31 - 3.35.
[4] R Haines-Young, C Watkins and C Lovers (1993), *Countryside Impacts Table: Final Report*, Department of Geography, University of Nottingham.

3.17   This project deals specifically with the effects of agriculture on the countryside. The goal was to develop a system that would inform policy advisers about the likely environmental consequences of changes in agricultural policy. This was to be achieved by bringing together the diverse scientific literature on the effects of different agricultural enterprises on the various components of the countryside and expressing its main conclusions in policy relevant terms.

3.18   In another study of the agriculture sector, the Centre for Agricultural Strategy at Reading University developed a linear programming model of agriculture in England and Wales,[1] designed to provide a quantitative and spatial analysis of the effects of policy changes on the agricultural sector. Their Land Use Allocation Model (LUAM) treats the agricultural sector as if it were a single farm employing a variety of different production activities and intensities which utilise, to varying degrees, inputs and resources (including different land types) to produce agricultural outputs. The principal data source used in the model's construction is the Farm Business Survey (FBS) - an annual survey of whole farm accounts from about 2,400 farms. These data are used to estimate input-output coefficients for agricultural enterprises. The spatial dimension is provided by allocating each farm in the data set to a land class according to the farm's location. The Land Classification System used for this purpose has been devised by the National Environmental Research Council's Institute for Terrestrial Ecology (ITE).

3.19   The model has the potential to be used in two modes: policy exogenous or policy endogenous. In the policy exogenous mode, agricultural policy (such as price levels, area payments, output and livestock quotas, set aside, etc) can be set and the consequences for the agricultural sector simulated in terms of production patterns, input usage and resource returns. Aggregate results can be analysed regionally or by the ITE land class. In principle, the model could be further developed to model more explicitly environmental and ecological implications. In the policy endogenous mode, natural environment objectives (eg reductions in fertiliser usage, types of ground cover, maximum stocking rates, etc) can be specified as inputs; the implications of these for agricultural returns are determined by the model. Comparison with a base situation shows the policy adjustments required to achieve the particular environmental objectives.

3.20   The model is currently being improved and updated using the most recent FBS and ITE data. This phase of the work is being funded

---

[1] Centre for Agricultural Strategy (1991), *Modelling Existing and Alternative Uses of Rural Land,* Report to the Ministry of Agriculture, Fisheries and Food.

by the Ministry of Agriculture, Fisheries and Food, the Department of the Environment, the Rural Development Commission and the Welsh Office and should be completed in September 1994.

Forestry

3.21   The Forestry Commission's main source of investment appraisal advice is their "Investment Appraisal Handbook".[1] It has recently been revised to give more guidance on the evaluation of non-market outputs. The revised Handbook incorporates recent case study material on the value of environmental benefits provided by forestry.   Details of valuation studies carried out for the Forestry Commission are summarised in Chapter IV.

3.22   An analysis of the economic and environmental costs and benefits of forestry expansion commissioned in 1990,[2] contributed significantly to the 1992 government restatement of forestry policy which promised that forestry expansion and management would in future be more directed towards multiple-use benefits.

3.23   The relationship between agriculture and forestry was an important feature of the "National Forest Cost-Benefit Analysis".[3] The National Forest project seeks to establish an area of attractive mixed woodland interspersed with agriculture and commercial and residential land use, over an area of 500 square kilometres in the English Midlands.

3.24   The cost-benefit analysis covers some difficult analytical issues such as the simulation of landowners' decisions to plant trees, and in appraising the effects of changes in farm and forestry production on private agents and on society as a whole. In the analysis, a landowner's decision whether or not to plant trees is modelled as a purely financial one. A given plot of land is switched into forestry as soon as the expected cash flow from doing so exceeds that from remaining in agriculture. Switching depends in a complex way on farm and timber prices, on the forest grants that are available, and on the rate of return that landowners expect.

3.25   Agriculture is a profitable activity for the landowners in the Forest area. Timber growing, on the other hand, is financially unattractive and existing forestry incentives are not sufficient to bring about enough planting to achieve the target tree cover.

---

[1] Forestry Commission (1987), *Investment Appraisal Handbook,* Forestry Commission.
[2] Forestry Commission (1992), *Forestry Expansion: A Study of Technical, Economic and Ecological Factors,* Forestry Commission Occasional Papers 33-47, Forestry Commission, Edinburgh.
[3] ibid.

3.26   Putting farming and forestry on an even footing, however, by comparing the value of their output at world trade prices without any subsidies, reveals that the net resource costs of switching into forestry are more than offset by landscape and recreational benefits. The estimation of these values is discussed in the next chapter (see below paras 4.17-4.26).

Land use planning: development plans

3.27   In 1992, the Department of the Environment produced guidance on how environmental concerns should be integrated into development plan preparation in its Planning Policy Guidance Note 12 (PPG12): "Development Plans and Regional Planning Guidance".[1] It also recommended that local planning authorities conduct an environmental appraisal of plans, policies and proposals as they are being drawn up.

3.28   During 1992, the Department commissioned research on environmental appraisal of development plans. The purpose of the research was:

i)   to look at environmental appraisal techniques currently being used;

ii)   to assess the effects of environmental appraisal on policy preparation;

iii)   to examine views about current advice (PPG12) on environmental appraisal; and

iv)   to advise on good practice techniques and procedures.

3.29   The project was carried out by a joint team from Baker Associates and the University of the West of England. It concluded that urgent guidance was required on how to implement the advice in PPG12. This led to the publication of "Environmental Appraisal of Development Plans: A Good Practice Guide"[2] at the end of 1993.

3.30   The Guide offers advice on a range of straightforward techniques and procedures on environmental appraisal. It shows the benefits arising from environmental appraisal and how they can be integrated into each stage of the plan-making process. The advice is not meant to be prescriptive. The framework and methodology can be easily used and adapted to a particular planning authority's circumstances

---

[1] Department of the Environment (1992), *Planning Policy Guidance: Development Plans and Regional Planning Guidance,* HMSO.

[2] Department of the Environment (1993) *The Environmental Appraisal of Development Plans: A Good Practice Guide,* HMSO.

and requirements. A full report on the research findings will be published during 1994.

Land use planning: projects

3.31   There are now well established procedures for assessing the environmental impacts of individual projects. They ensure that information about the likely effects of a project on the environment is collected, assessed and available to the authority charged with deciding whether the development should go ahead. This includes identifying adverse effects and ways in which such effects might be avoided or mitigated.

3.32   A joint Department of the Environment/Welsh Office booklet on environmental assessment[1] gives advice on the environmental assessment of projects. This is intended primarily for developers and their advisers. It explains how requirements for the environmental assessment of certain types of projects which are likely to have significant environmental effects have been incorporated into consent procedures in the UK. This follows implementation of the EC Directive on "The assessment of the effects of certain public and private projects on the environment" (85/337/EEC) which came into effect in July 1988.

3.33   In 1993, the Department of the Environment, the Scottish Office Environment Department and the Welsh Office commissioned Land Use Consultants, together with the Environmental Appraisal Group of the University of East Anglia, to carry out research to enable the departments to produce a good practice guide to assist local authorities in England, Scotland and Wales in their appraisal of "environmental information". This is information which must be taken into account when determining planning applications which are the subject of an environmental statement (ES).

3.34   The purpose of the research was to review existing literature and experience, including monetary and non-monetary valuation techniques, and to prepare draft guidance to assist planning authorities:

(i)   to consider whether submitted ESs are adequate or whether additional information needs to be sought from the applicants; and

(ii)   to appraise the information in the ES and any representations from statutory consultees and others, so that this can contribute to an informed decision on the application for planning permission.

---

[1] Department of the Environment/Welsh Office (1989), *Environmental Assessment: A Guide to the Procedures,* HMSO.

20

3.35   Preliminary findings of the research suggest that, in general, planning authorities do not use formal methods and techniques to appraise environmental information where projects are subject to EA. That is not to say that such methods and techniques do not have a role to play and, although no one approach should be regarded as a panacea, there are a number which might be employed to clarify specific areas of uncertainty. Their usefulness is likely to be enhanced if they are initiated at an early stage of an EA study; they are easily understood and simple to use; and they do not involve substantial time and expense.

Transport

3.36   Directive 85/337/EEC requires an environmental assessment to be carried out for transport projects likely to have significant effects on the environment.

3.37   In 1993, the Department of Transport (jointly with the Welsh Office, the Scottish Office and the Department of the Environment for Northern Ireland) published updated and expanded guidance on the environmental assessment of new and improved trunk roads, including motorways, in Volume 11 of the "Design Manual for Roads and Bridges".[1]   This replaced previous guidance in the Manual of Environmental Appraisal (which applied to England and Wales) and parts of the Scottish Traffic and Environmental Appraisal Manual.

3.38   Volume 11 formalises assessment procedures at three key stages in the development of trunk road projects: before entry to the trunk road programme; at public consultation; and by publication of an Environmental Statement. It will be updated as necessary.

3.39   Volume 5 of the Design Manual for Roads and Bridges[2] was also published in 1993. This requires environmental assessments to be co-ordinated with engineering and economic assessments at the three key stages and fed into the decision making process.

3.40   Mitigation is an integral part of the design and planning of a scheme. Assessment and design are considered as an iterative process. Guidance on environmental design is given in "The Good Roads Guide" which is included in Volume 10 of the Design Manual for Roads and Bridges.[3] This gives advice on the best practice in landscaping and environmental treatment of trunk roads. This too was published in 1993.

---

[1] Department of Transport (1993), *Design Manual for Roads and Bridges: Volume 11 - Environmental Assessment,* HMSO.

[2] Department of Transport (1993), *Design Manual for Roads and Bridges: Volume 5 - Assessment and Preparation of Road Schemes,* HMSO.

[3] Department of Transport (1993), *Design Manual for Roads and Bridges: Volume 10 - Environmental Design,* HMSO.

Channel Tunnel Rail Link

3.41   Although these documents have been prepared for use with trunk road schemes, their principles (as opposed to the detailed advice) are relevant to the appraisal of other transport infrastructure.

3.42   An example of an environmental appraisal of a major transport infrastructure is the Channel Tunnel Rail Link. The development of the route for high speed rail services between the Channel Tunnel and London has been a staged process with each stage including successively more detailed environmental studies. In October 1991, the Government announced a preferred approach to central London which had been selected from four main options. Union Railways were asked to prepare for public consultation a "Reference Case" route which would maximise the return to the project, whilst meeting the environmental standards generally applied to other major transport infrastructure projects.

3.43   Union Railways commissioned Environmental Resources Management (ERM) to undertake environmental appraisals at each stage of the route development process. ERM provided Union Railways and the Government with an independent environmental appraisal to inform the decision making process, commensurate with the level of detail that the engineering design had reached. This was used to compare route options and to identify potential problems.

3.44   The environmental appraisals so far carried out constitute the early stage of the environmental assessment process. The production of an Environmental Statement (ES) as required by EC Directive 85/337/EEC will be the final stage of the process, and will report the results of a comprehensive assessment of the environmental impacts of the project. The ES will be completed now that the Government has announced its decision on the route and will be published when the project goes to Parliament for approval.

3.45   The methodology used for this study is described in the box on page 24. The environmental appraisal raised two "major" and 23 "high moderate" concerns. Excluding those for possible intermediate station sites, this is an average of one every 4.5 kilometres, a reasonable rate given the populous and environmentally sensitive nature of the areas affected by the route in London, Essex and Kent.

3.46   The two "major" concerns were the effect of the route on an Area of Outstanding Natural Beauty west of the River Medway and the amount of high quality agricultural land to be taken. Both of these concerns were mitigated by adoption of a route variant closer to an existing motorway, though this solution was more expensive and entails ecological costs of its own.

3.47   Two issues of "high moderate" concern about noise and settlement effects were raised in the London section. These are now to be avoided by following the "St Pancras Alternative" which has fewer environmental impacts than the Reference Case.

3.48   The route is being refined further in the light of public consultation. Localised design changes and additional mitigation measures will be incorporated in the scheme, as far as is practicable, to address the remaining significant environmental concerns.

METHODOLOGY FOR CHANNEL TUNNEL RAIL LINK STUDY

The design and environmental teams worked closely together. The three step process for the development of the route is described below. The appraisal processes used for other stages in the project development are broadly similar.

Option Definition The teams identified, modified and rejected route options as they defined ways to traverse the route. Environmental Features Mapping (EFM) provided the baseline information on built-up areas, agriculture, contaminated land, ecology, groundwater features, historic and cultural features, and landscape features. EFM data were used by the design team to complete the environmental elements of an option proforma which was then validated by the environmental team.

Option Development Design teams developed options carried forward from the previous stage. A framework, completed by engineering design teams and validated by specialist environmental assessment consultants (EACs), was applied. Input from this was supplemented by appraisals by EACs. Options were rejected which were environmentally unacceptable by major UK infrastructure standards.

An environmental ranking of the various route options within each route section was established. Consideration of the effects on people and on resources was used to create a preference tree of sub-route options. This allowed the derivation of "hybrid" routes, combining lengths from a number of options.

Option Appraisal Environmental input was made using the full environmental appraisal framework, supplemented by appraisals by EACs. Effects were categorised into those being of:

* **major concern:** probability of issue alone leading to refusal was greater than 50%

* **moderate concern, split between high moderate and low moderate:** issue unlikely to cause refusal on its own, but could be one of several issues together leading to refusal

* **minor concern:** issue can be resolved through mitigation and consultation.

Transport policy alternatives

a) A470 Corridor Study

3.49   The environmental impact of road transport has focused attention, inter alia, on the extent to which public transport can, in some instances, provide more attractive options. An example of such a study is the A470 corridor public transport study.[1] This was commissioned by the Secretary of State for Wales to investigate options for improving public transport to provide traffic relief for the A470 corridor in South Wales at a lower cost than the £50 million for highway improvements identified in an earlier study.

3.50   Several public transport options were scrutinised individually and in various combinations. The options were: enhancement of the existing Valley Lines heavy rail system; light rail transit; busways or bus lanes; and guided bus systems.

3.51   Conversion of the whole of the Valley Lines heavy rail network to light rail operation was rejected largely on the grounds of cost, as was guided light transport (GLT) technology. Track sharing, however, remained a possibility. One of the three options identified for detailed consideration was enhanced heavy rail services with complementary light rail services introduced between Cardiff and suitable interchanges. The other two options were: enhanced heavy rail services that were faster and more frequent than current services; and enhanced heavy rail services with a complementary kerb guided busway using diesel buses between Cardiff and suitable interchanges.

3.52   The appraisal suggested that only the enhanced heavy rail option gave a positive financial return. But the impact of these substantial public transport improvements on A470 traffic conditions was of paramount importance. A full cost-benefit study was therefore undertaken to estimate the value of user and non-user benefits, namely savings in travel time, savings in vehicle operating costs, and savings in accident costs. The incidence of visual intrusion and disruption during construction, the effects upon properties and ecologically-sensitive areas, and the implications for energy consumption were also noted.

3.53   The results of the cost-benefit study showed that all three options had positive net present values. The study concluded, however, that public transport investment alone would not attract a sufficient number of car users to preclude the need for highway improvements to the A470 corridor in the near future.

---

[1] JMP Consultants (1993), *A470 Corridor Public Transport Study*, Report for the Welsh Office.

b) Public transport options for the environment

3.54   The responsibility for developing strategies to deal with local transport problems rests, outside London, primarily with local authorities. Central government gives local authorities the necessary approvals for borrowing to finance transport investment, and provides direct grants in certain circumstances. It also has a role in giving planning guidance, carrying out research and disseminating best practice. To assist it in this role, the Urban and General Directorate of the Department of Transport has commissioned from the Department's Transport Research Laboratory two research projects under the study heading "Public Transport Options for the Environment".

3.55   The objective of this research has been to estimate the impact of fiscal and physical policy measures, applied at a city-wide level, on road traffic and emissions levels in cities of varying size and form. Information on these impacts, and on how different policy options perform in cities with differing demographic and spatial characteristics, will assist the Department in understanding better the nature of the interaction between various measures to alleviate urban traffic congestion, and the case for major policy measures such as urban congestion charging, or controls on private non-residential parking, which would require new legislation. The options considered include both "carrot" measures to improve the attractiveness of public transport, and "stick" measures to restrain road traffic directly.

3.56   This work has involved the construction of models of travel behaviour and traffic flows in urban areas based on data from a number of cities. Phase I of the study, completed in 1990, developed a simple model of travel behaviour in a medium sized English city of roughly 500,000 population. In Phase II of the study (September 1991 - October 1993), the model developed for Phase I was compared with two alternative models. The original model was then used for policy testing on a further four cities with differing characteristics. The results of these tests were then compared with those obtained for the city which was originally modelled in Phase I.

3.57   The range of policies considered in Phase II was slightly different from that in Phase I. Complexities of modelling meant that it was too difficult to model the effects of a multi-line light rail (LRT) network but congestion charging was added to the range of direct road traffic restraint measures.

3.58   The Phase I study concluded that even extensive improvement to public transport, including the construction of new light rail lines had a much smaller effect on emissions than policies which directl discouraged the use of cars. Such policies included greater restrictions on parking, and options for cordon charging. The study also suggested that city centre traffic restraint options, although leading to significant transfers of trips to public transport, would lead to a reduction in total trip-making to the city centre. This outcome is inconsistent with central and local government policies to preserve and enhance the economic vitality of city centres. The model showed, however, that this effect on total trip-making could be at least partially offset by the addition of measures to make public transport more attractive.

3.59   The Phase II study has largely confirmed these findings, and has suggested that congestion charging would be at least as effective in reducing emissions as radical parking restraint measures. There are, however, important differences between cities in the modelled effects of the same policies on trip patterns, road speeds and emissions.

3.60   Decisions at both local and national government level on fiscal and physical aspects of urban transport policy cannot be taken exclusively on the basis of a few environmental indicators produced by models such as those developed for this study. Wider considerations, such as the economic and financial performance of the policies and the impact on the urban economy, as well as the results of more detailed modelling, need to be taken into account. These and other issues are being addressed in the Department's study of city congestion charging for London. A report of the findings will be published.

Water

3.61   The National Rivers Authority (NRA) has an economic appraisal manual[1] which is designed to help ensure effective management of public funds. It describes the different stages of an appraisal, and discusses the valuation methods that could be used to estimate the costs and benefits of NRA activities. It also includes practical examples of studies where the techniques have been used and provides some very general 'look-up' tables. The structure and comprehensive nature of the manual makes it a useful reference manual for economic appraisals involving river quality, river flows and flood defence protection.

3.62   The Regulators and Water Operators are currently funding a research project[2] to produce a benefit assessment manual with the best practical tools for assessing the benefits of improved river quality. The project is divided into two stages: an interim manual is planned at the end of the first phase and a final manual at the end of the second.

---

[1] National Rivers Authority (forthcoming), *Economic Appraisal Manual,* NRA.

[2] The project is managed by the Foundation for Water Research (FWR); it is spread over three years commencing 1993/4.

3.63   The interim manual will concentrate on assessing the benefits of improved river quality on angling, informal recreation, drinking water supplies and non-use benefits. It will include general information on cost-benefit analysis and step-by-step instructions on how to identify and estimate the above benefits using look-up tables and formulae.

3.64   The final manual will refine some of the estimates provided in the interim manual. The range of benefit categories will also be extended to include boating, immersion water sports and benefits to agriculture, industry and property development.

Flood and coastal defence; sea level rise

3.65   Recent surveys of sea defences in England and Wales carried out by the NRA have shown that there are some 300 kilometres of sea defences in England and Wales providing flood protection to urban land and a further 960 kilometres of defences protecting mainly rural and agricultural land from flooding from the sea. Some of these rural defences protect very large land areas; they include 57% of the country's grade 1 agricultural land.

3.66   Applications to the Ministry of Agriculture, Fisheries and Food for grant aid for flood and coastal defence works have to be prepared in accordance with the Ministry's "Flood and Coastal Defence: Project Appraisal Guidance Notes".[1]   These notes, which are designed to help authorities make better decisions and to achieve greater value for money, replace the earlier (1985) publication, "Investment Appraisal of Arterial Drainage, Flood Protection and Sea Defence Schemes: Guidance for Drainage Authorities".[2]

3.67   A research project at Middlesex University funded by the Ministry of Agriculture, Fisheries and Food has developed techniques which allow some of the intangible benefits of flood and coastal defence, including environmental benefits, to be valued. The project led to the publication in September 1992 of "The Economics of Coastal Management"[3] which has become known as the Yellow Manual. It complements "Urban Flood Protection Benefits"[4] and "The Benefits of Flood Alleviation"[5] known as the Red and Blue Manuals respectively.

[1] Ministry of Agriculture, Fisheries and Food (1993), *Flood and Coastal Defence: Project Appraisal Guidance Notes,* HMSO.
[2] Ministry of Agriculture, Fisheries and Food (1985), *Investment Appraisal of Arterial Drainage, Flood Protection and Sea Defence Schemes: Guidance for Drainage Authorities*, HMSO.
[3] E C Penning-Rowsell, C H Green, P M Thompson, A M Coker, S M Tunstall, C Richards and D J Parker (1992), *The Economics of Coastal Management: A Manual of Benefits Assessment Techniques* Belhaven Press.
[4] D J Parker, C H Green and P M Thompson (1987), *Urban Flood Protection Benefits, A Project Appraisal Guide*, Gower.
[5] Ministry of Agriculture, Fisheries and Food (1993), *Benefits of Flood Alleviation*, MAFF.

3.68   A case study of vulnerability to accelerated sea level rise for the East Anglian coastal zone was carried out by the University of East Anglia.[1]

3.69   The main risks posed by accelerated sea level rise (ASLR) in this hazard zone are from increased flooding and coastal erosion. The output of 1990/91 global climatological models, based on the work of the Intergovernmental Panel on Climate Change (IPCC) and their predictions of ASLR, established the baselines for the estimation of the potential hazard.

3.70   The case study methodology included the following stages:

(i)   the development of regional scenarios of ASLR;

(ii) the development of analysis linking ASLR with specific physical hazards - flooding, inundation and erosion;

(iii) the collection of data about the assets at risk;

(iv) the assessment of response options;

(v)   the economic appraisals of the costs and benefits of the various response options.

3.71   In order to identify the most economically efficient responses, the study considered the range of policy response options, including "do nothing", "maintain current defence levels" and "improve defences as sea levels rise".

3.72   The costs of each option were calculated for some 210 kilometres of the East Anglian coastline. The basic approach was to combine information about the physical hazard posed by ASLR with data on assets at risk, in order to produce physical and economic estimates of the impacts of ASLR.

Climate change

3.73   A study, carried out by National Economic Research Associates (NERA) for the Department of the Environment and the Department of Trade and Industry, investigated the implications for trade and competitiveness, in the major producing and consuming countries of the OECD, of greenhouse gas emissions control and, in particular, of countries adopting different emissions control targets and instruments.[2]

3.74   The research examined the operation of individual measures at the micro-economic level; their likely impact on the pattern of energy

---

[1] University of East Anglia (1991), *Economic Appraisal of Climate Induced Sea Level Rise: A Case Study of East Anglia*, UEA.

[2] National Economic Research Associates (1991), *Links Between Environmental and International Trade Policies*.

use; the operation of the global economy; and the legal framework under which international trade is conducted. To simplify matters, the consultants chose:

(i) to provide an illustration of a theoretical discussion of individual measures with a single country energy model;

(ii) to simulate the strategic behaviour of an imperfectly competitive industry faced with varying emissions measures;

(iii) to discuss the global impact of likely scenarios by making use of world fuel and macro economic-models; and

(iv) to address the trade policy questions raised.

3.75   The global emissions reduction scenarios did not generally seem to give large gains to free riders. "Emissions leakages" of the order of 25% were predicted. The report's discussion of trade policy concludes that the scope for using it to enforce environmental agreements is limited and runs the risk of encouraging protectionism.

Hazardous chemicals

3.76   The widespread use of chemicals in the modern world has led to increasing concern over possible effects upon both people and the environment. For substances which have been identified as having the potential to cause long term damage, there is a range of existing controls. A recent study developed a methodology for appraising regulatory control options.[1]

3.77   The methodology used is a form of cost-benefit analysis known as risk-benefit analysis. This approach balances environmental and human health risks against the benefits associated with the use of a given hazardous substance. The costs and benefits of a regulatory decision are made explicit.

3.78   The methodology was applied in case studies of two chemicals: tributyltin (TBT) and polybrominated diphenyl ethers (PBDE's). TBT is used as a wood preservative and also as a marine anti-fouling paint where it can damage the aquatic environment. PBDE's are used as flame retardants in plastics and furnishing fabrics, and there is concern over their potential to generate poisonous dioxins and furans.

3.79   Despite data deficiencies which made it difficult to assess the efficacy of substitute chemicals or to quantify environmental and

---

[1] Risk and Policy Analysts in association with Acer Environmental (1992), *Risk Benefit Analysis o[f] Hazardous Chemicals,* Report for the Department of the Environment.

human health risks, it was possible to draw some conclusions about the implications of bans on the use of these chemicals.

3.80   For TBT, it was estimated that the cost to shipowners currently using UK dry docks of using alternative paints would be about £50 million. To justify a ban, therefore, the value of damage to shellfish and associated ecosystems from continued use of TBT would have to amount to at least this sum.

3.81   The cost to industry and consumers in the textile sector of banning the use of PBDE's and of finding a suitable alternative was estimated at £150 million, equivalent to a 2.5% increase in upholstered furniture costs. A ban in the textile sector would therefore be justified if the value of damage to human health from continued use of PBDE's was greater than this sum.

3.82   The methodology involves the following stages:

(i)   the identification of the key issues surrounding the problem and the key impacts requiring analysis;

(ii)   the collection of base data on production and   consumption of the chemicals and on potential   substitutes;

(iii)   the identification of the stages at which releases might occur;

(iv)   the assessment of the environmental risks associated with production, use and disposal of the chemicals;

(v)   the assessment of the human health effects associated with the chemicals;

(vi)   the estimation of relevant costs and benefits of different regulatory controls, including private costs and benefits (changes in producer and consumer surplus) and external (environmental and health) costs and benefits; and

(vii)   the appraisal of the trade-offs between risks and costs under different control assumptions.

3.83   The risk-benefit analysis of hazardous substances is now the subject of a working group consisting jointly of officials and representatives of the Chemical Industries Association. This working group aims to publish guidance later this year.

Waste management   3.84   The UK is currently taking part in the negotiation of a proposed EC Directive for packaging and packaging waste. The principal aims of the proposed Directive are: to reduce the impact of packaging and packaging waste on the environment; and to prevent the single market being distorted by unilateral national measures.

3.85   The Department of Trade and Industry has commissioned a study into the costs to industry of complying with the Directive under various scenarios.[1]   The consultants were also asked to provide an overview of the implications of the Directive for the competitiveness of UK industry.

3.86   The methodology used to estimate the compliance costs takes account of the wide-ranging nature of the Directive's effects. The costs which would be imposed by the Directive are assessed using three possible methods of implementation. The three possible scenarios examined are as follows:

(i)   collection, sorting and recycling are market driven;

(ii)   collection and sorting are market driven, but the recycling is centrally controlled; and

(iii) collection, sorting and recycling are all   centrally controlled.

3.87   The costs for each of these three scenarios are then compared to a "base case" which represents the situation most likely to arise in the packaging industry in the absence of a Directive. The assessment of costs and competitiveness effects involved an extensive process of consultation.

3.88   The consultants calculate the costs to UK industry of managing packaging waste at the target levels as £7.8 billion - base case. The costs incurred under the proposed Directive, however, range from £9.9 billion for scenarios (i) and (ii) to £10.4 billion for (iii). An additional annual cost of £2.1 - £2.6 billion more than in the base case can therefore be expected.

3.89   The consultants noted that the cost burden is not evenly distributed between the key industries. For example, around 50% of the additional costs under all three scenarios will be borne by the plastics sector, where significant investment in new plant will be required to meet the proposed EC targets.

---

[1] David Perchard Associates and KPMG Management Consultants (1992), *EC Directive on Packaging and Packaging Waste,* Report to the Department of Trade and Industry.

3.90   The CCA was prepared on the basis of the EC Commission's original proposal for the Directive which embodied very high targets for the recovery and recycling of packaging waste. In December 1993, the Environment Council finally agreed significantly lower recovery and recycling targets. Consequently, the costs that will be incurred are likely to be very much lower than those suggested by the CCA.

References

Centre for Agricultural Strategy (1991), *Modelling Existing and Alternative Uses of Rural Land,* Report to the Ministry of Agriculture, Fisheries and Food.

CSERGE, Warren Spring Laboratory, EFTEC (1993), *Externalities from Landfill and Incineration*, Report to the Department of the Environment, HMSO.

Department of the Environment and the Welsh Office (1989), *Environmental Assessment: A Guide to the Procedures*, HMSO.

Department of the Environment (1992), *Planning Policy Guidance: Development Plans and Regional Planning Guidance,* HMSO.

Department of the Environment (1992), *This Common Inheritance: The Second Year Report*, HMSO.

Department of the Environment (1993), *The Environmental Appraisal of Development Plans: A Good Practice Guide,* HMSO.

Department of Transport (1993), *Design Manual for Roads and Bridges: Volume 5 - Assessment and Preparation of Road Schemes,* HMSO.

Department of Transport (1993), *Design Manual for Roads and Bridges: Volume 10 - Environmental Design,* HMSO.

Department of Transport (1993), *Design Manual for Roads and Bridges: Volume 11 - Environmental Assessment,* HMSO.

K Field, B Shoderu and C Normand (1993), *Cost Effectiveness of Measures to Reduce Radon in Existing Dwellings,* Report for the Department of the Environment.

Forestry Commission (1987), *Investment Appraisal Handbook*, Forestry Commission.

Forestry Commission (1992), *Forestry Expansion: A Study of Technical, Economic and Ecological factors,* Forestry Commission Occasional Papers 33-47, Forestry Commission, Edinburgh.

R Haines-Young, C Watkins and C Lovers (1993), *Countryside Impacts Table: Final Report*, Department of Geography, University of Nottingham.

HM Government (1994), *Sustainable Development: The UK Strategy,* HMSO.

JMP Consultants (1993), *A470 Corridor Public Transport Study*, Report for the Welsh Office.

London Economics (1992), *The Potential Role of Market Mechanisms in the Control of Acid Rain*, HMSO.

London Economics (1993), *National Forest Cost-Benefit Analysis*, unpublished report for the Countryside Commission.

Ministry of Agriculture, Fisheries and Food (1985), *Investment Appraisal of Arterial Drainage, Flood Protection and Sea Defence Schemes: Guidance for Drainage Authorities*, HMSO.

Ministry of Agriculture, Fisheries and Food (1993), *Flood and Coastal Defence: Project Appraisal Guidance Notes*, HMSO.

Ministry of Agriculture, Fisheries and Food (1993), *Benefits of Flood Alleviation*, MAFF.

National Economic Research Associates (1991), *Links Between Environmental and International Trade Policies.*

National Rivers Authority (forthcoming), *Economic Appraisal Manual*, NRA.

D J Parker, C H Green and P M Thompson (1987), *Urban Flood Protection Benefits: A Project Appraisal Guide*, Gower.

E C Penning-Rowsell, C H Green, P M Thompson, A M Coker, S M Tunstall, C Richards and D J Parker (1992), *The Economics of Coastal Management: A Manual of Benefits Assessment Techniques*, Belhaven Press.

David Perchard Associates, KPMG Management Consulting, *EC Directive on Packaging and Packaging Waste, Compliance Cost Assessment*, Report for the Department of Trade and Industry.

J Pezzey (1991), *Impacts of Greenhouse Gas Control Strategies on UK Competitiveness*, HMSO.

Risk and Policy Analysts in association with Acer Environmental (1992), *Risk-Benefit Analysis of Hazardous Chemicals*, Report for the Department of the Environment.

University of East Anglia (1991), *Economic Appraisal of Climate Induced Sea Level Rise: A Case Study of East Anglia*, UEA.

Chapter 4: Environmental Valuation Studies

Introduction

4.1 The purpose of this chapter is briefly to summarise some work on monetary valuation that has been commissioned by government departments. Three general criteria guide the decision on whether to undertake a monetary valuation exercise. These are:

(i) whether a conceptually sensible way forward can be found;

(ii) whether the required data are available or can be made available;

(iii) how expensive a valuation study is likely to be in terms of skilled manpower, etc in relation to the intrinsic importance of the issue to be addressed.

4.2 The expertise available for carrying out environmental valuation exercises is, in the UK, concentrated in a relatively small number of university departments. In particular, the ESRC's initiatives in financing the Countryside Change Initiative at Newcastle University and the Centre for Social and Economic Research on the Global Environment (CSERGE) at University College, London and the University of East Anglia have, to some extent, reflected and encouraged the concentration of expertise.

4.3 It would however be wrong to assume that there are no alternatives to sophisticated valuation exercises of the kind undertaken by these institutions. Useful input may take the form of informed calculations of value and/or of sensitivity analyses exploring the implications of a range of hypothetical values.

4.4 The first case study considered below is a literature review. The other case studies summarised provide examples of three kinds of research: first, scoping studies to determine the feasibility of monetary valuation in particular areas of policy and the methodology to be used; second, studies that provide "rough and ready" estimates of environmental value falling short of sophisticated surveys or economic analysis; third, there are the full blown valuation studies themselves.

The social costs of fuel cycles

4.5   Research carried out in 1992 for the Department of Trade and Industry by the Centre for Social and Economic Research on the Global Environment (CSERGE)[1] was designed to survey the available literature on the monetary valuation of the social costs of electricity generation fuel cycles; and, in particular, to elicit any consensus about externalities (e.g. social costs and benefits).

4.6   The research considered a number of different fuel cycles including conventional coal-fired power stations, advanced coal-fired systems, combined cycle gas turbines, nuclear power (using pressurised water reactors), wind energy, landfill gas, geothermal energy, tidal power, hydro-electric power, wave energy, solar energy, and combined heat and power and municipal solid waste plant.

4.7   The term "fuel cycle" was taken to encompass the complete set of activities associated with the production of a unit of electricity. For example, in the case of nuclear power, this included the mining of the uranium ore through to fuel fabrication, power generation, reprocessing, waste disposal and plant decommissioning. Since social costs are incurred at various stages of the fuel cycle for each energy source, impacts were investigated at each stage. Where possible, the report attempted to derive preliminary estimates of social costs and to show how these might be converted to "externality adders" applicable to UK electricity generation fuel cycles.

4.8   During the course of the research, it became apparent that, while a great deal of work had been undertaken on the coal and nuclear electricity fuel cycles, there was little, if any, on many of the other fuels. There was also considerable variation in the quality and comprehensiveness of the available research on the individual environmental impacts. In particular, there were few studies on the amenity impacts of energy activities. The report acknowledged the uncertainties in estimating monetary values for environmental damage. Some illustrative figures were presented for the various fuel cycles examined.

Stated preference scoping study

4.9   One of the statutory functions of Scottish Enterprise is to further the improvement of the environment of Scotland. In this and other contexts the organisation is responsible for ensuring that projects are adequately appraised, and that appropriate methodologies and techniques are developed to assist the appraisal process. Scottish Enterprise is now trying to develop a usable environmental appraisal system. This includes the identification, quantification and valuation of environmental impacts.

---

[1] D W Pearce and C Bann (1992), *Social Costs of Fuel Cycles,* HMSO.

4.10   In a follow-up to the earlier work by Nick Hanley and ECOTEC Ltd[1], Scottish Enterprise has undertaken a scoping exercise[2] to consider whether the stated preference technique could be applied to environmental valuation and, if so, to design and pilot a series of questionnaires to address the main types of environmental projects undertaken by Scottish Enterprise.

4.11   Scottish Enterprise is currently undertaking further development work on stated preference techniques, in particular in the context of town centre schemes. This research involves a number of stated preference investigations of large environmental projects; the results obtained are being compared with those generated by alternative techniques; the transferability of stated preference results across different projects with similar components is being examined; and appropriate survey questionnaire templates and guidance is being provided on the types of projects most suitable for the application of the stated preference technique.

The value of biodiversity in UK forests

4.12   A scoping study carried out for the Forestry Commission by Environmental Resources Ltd (now Environmental Resources Management Ltd) concerned the value of biodiversity in UK forests.[3]

4.13   Enhancement of forest biodiversity involves making trade-offs between management for biodiversity and other objectives of forestry: commercial production of timber; amenity and recreation, etc. The policy question is how to allocate forest land for different objectives. Valuation of biodiversity has a potentially central role to play in making informed decisions about the trade-offs to be made.

4.14   Before any resource can be valued, it first needs to be measured and quantified in physical terms. The techniques are not yet available to do this for the general category of "biodiversity". Considerable progress is, however, being made in the field of forestry towards developing indicators which may form the basis for units of account for biodiversity. The consultants concluded that, if such indicators were to be developed, the contingent valuation method might then be used. This might be supported by other approaches, such as the use of expert groups to categorise or rank different types of biodiversity.

---

[1] N Hanley in association with ECOTEC Ltd, *The Valuation of Environmental Effects, Stages I and II*. Final reports published by the Scottish Office Industry Department/Scottish Enterprise as *ESU Research Papers No.22* (1990) and *No.27* (1992).

[2] Report by a Panel of Consultants (1993), *Stated Preference Scoping Study,* Report for Scottish Enterprise.

[3] Environmental Resources Limited (1993), *The Valuation of Biodiversity in UK Forests*, Report for the Forestry Commission.

4.15   If, in practice, quantitative measures (derived from indicators based on a wide set of factors) cannot be developed, then analysis will need to be based on simpler measures, such as the number of species and the size of population of each.   Under such circumstances, techniques such as portfolio analysis offer interesting potential as a means of examining the trade-off between commercial timber value and the risk of loss of species or habitats across a range of forest types.

4.16   Another approach would use cost-effectiveness analysis to achieve targets for biodiversity in UK forests.   Such policy targets could be based on concepts such as safe minimum standards or minimum viable population.   The central problem with these concepts is that they constrain the ability to make trade-offs as they effectively attribute infinite value to species until the point at which the target is reached and zero value thereafter.   Also, they provide no mechanism for valuing the existence of additional species or increases in the population of the different species.   Measurement would still be needed in order to establish and maintain the target population or standard.

Forest recreation and amenity

4.17   The valuation of biodiversity presents particularly difficult analytical problems.   More amenable to economic analysis are the recreational and amenity benefits associated with forests.[1]

4.18   In 1991/92, the Policy Studies Division of the Forestry Commission carried out a cost-benefit analysis of three forests within the joint Countryside Commission/Forestry Commission Community Forest Initiative (Forest of Mercia, Great North Forest, Thames Chase). This examined planting proposals for each of the forests, and calculated their associated financial costs and benefits.   An attempt was also made to estimate the non-financial benefits which might arise from the creation of the forests.

4.19   The value of recreation and landscape improvement in the forests was estimated by a contingent valuation study conducted during January 1992.   A thousand randomly selected people living within each of the forest areas and up to five miles outside, were sent a two-page note describing what the initiative was trying to do and containing pictures to demonstrate what the forests might look like when they were planted.   Shortly after this, the contingent valuation survey took place and collected information about individuals' preferences for the countryside and for the new forests, and probed their willingness to pay for the creation of the forests.

---

[1] Forestry Commission (1993), *The Costs and Benefits of Planting Three Community Forests: Forest of Mercia, Thames Chase and Great North Forest*, Forestry Commission.

4.20   Residents generally said they were willing to pay £7.50-£9.50 per year for the creation of the forests. Dividing this by the estimated number of visits respondents said they would make on average, these figures were roughly equivalent to a value of 50p per visit. Validity testing indicated that these results were in the reasonable bounds of plausibility that are usually obtained in contingent valuation studies. Because individuals were shown photographs of what the forests would look like in their mature state, it was decided to assume that these figures would only be applicable to mature crops. The recreational benefits that might be obtained during the early years of establishment were scaled back accordingly.

4.21   By multiplying the stated benefits by the estimated populations living within and up to five miles outside the community forests, and adjusting for the gradual build-up in use (related to the age of crops) and gradual planting of the forest, the total non-market recreation and landscape value of the forests was estimated at £12-19 million. This did not take into account any recreation value that might be obtained by individuals living more than five miles away.

4.22   The contingent valuation estimates derived for the Community Forest Initiative have subsequently been used by London Economics in their National Forest Cost-Benefit Analysis (see above paras 3.23-3.26).

4.23   The tourism study undertaken for the National Forest estimates that, at its peak in about 20 years' time, the Forest will attract half a million staying visitors, and 5.4 million day trippers per year. This would be about half the number of visitors currently enjoying the New Forest in Hampshire and would be 7% and 11% respectively of the numbers of staying visitors and day trippers in the East Midlands in 1990. Forest area residents would be visiting the Forest, on average, about nine times a year.

4.24   These visitors will undoubtedly enjoy benefits from the Forest, but how much will it be worth to them? In the absence of a full blown survey of National Forest visitors, the consultants used the contingent valuation estimates derived for the Community Forest Initiative. The application of these figures indicated net present values of £7 million for staying visitors and £31 million for day trippers.

4.25   The National Forest will also improve the quality of landscape and thus bring benefits to residents in the area even if they make no active use of it. To measure this benefit, the analysis looked at the change in house prices the Forest will induce in the Leicestershire Midland Coalfield. This is a part of the Forest area with little tree cover and scarred by opencast coal mining, whose landscape will be transformed for the better by the project. The idea is that the prices of houses in areas of attractive landscape will exceed those in less attractive areas, and that the price difference will reflect the value of the benefit the household attaches to the landscape difference.

4.26   The change in house prices was estimated in three ways: from econometric studies of the effect of forests elsewhere in the UK; from local estate agents' estimates of likely changes in response to the Forest; and by comparing the Coalfield area with Charnwood, an area of the Forest whose already attractive landscape will not be significantly altered by the project. The full effects of the change in house prices will not be realised until most of the planting has been completed, that is in about twenty years. The consensus of these approaches was that the present value of the price increase will be about 2%. As the value of the housing stock in the Coalfield area in 1991 was about £1500 million, this suggests an estimated net present value of benefits of £30 million.

Environmentally Sensitive Areas (ESAs)

4.27   The need to assess the benefits of Environmentally Sensitive Area (ESA) agreements has prompted one of the largest contingent valuation studies yet undertaken in Europe.[1] ESA agreements are designed to conserve the landscape and protect the environment from intensive farming practices, by compensating farmers for income they forgo in following environmentally sensitive practices. This study, by the Centre for Rural Economy at the University of Newcastle-upon-Tyne for the Ministry of Agriculture, Fisheries and Food, sought to attach monetary values to the public benefits of two ESAs - the Somerset Levels and Moors ESA and the South Downs ESA. The study identified two alternative scenarios. First, the "without ESA" scenario is that which would have ensued given the continuation of intensive agriculture in these areas after 1987, but allowing for some amelioration under the MacSharry proposals for CAP reform. Second, the "with ESA" scenario: the landscape impacts of ESA agreements and payment levels between 1987 and 1992 continuing into the future.

4.28   The benefits to the public produced by ESA agreements can be broadly categorised as landscape, wildlife, and archaeological/historical preservation values. The Somerset Levels and Moors ESA aims to maintain the area of grassland and increase its diversity and value as a nesting ground for birds, and protect and upgrade landscape features like willows and ditches. The South Downs ESA aims to protect the remaining areas of downland pastures, to revert arable land to pasture

---

[1] K G Willis, G D Garrod and C M Saunders (1993), *Valuation of the South Downs and Somerset Levels and Moors Environmentally Sensitive Area Landscapes by the General Public*, Report for the Ministry of Agriculture, Fisheries and Food.

and encourage greater floral diversity, and to protect river valleys and archaeological features.

4.29 The net benefits of ESA landscapes are defined in the study as the difference between having the ESAs and not having the ESAs. These accrue to three groups in society: people living within ESAs; visitors to ESAs; and the rest of the general public. Benefits to residents and visitors are user values. The general public may derive benefits (existence values) from knowing such landscapes, wildlife habitats, and historic features are being protected.

4.30 The principal objectives of the study were therefore:

(i) to determine the public's ranking of alternative landscapes in the South Downs and Somerset Levels and Moors ESAs and to estimate the benefits of the different ESA landscapes - for both users (visitors and residents) and non-users (rest of the general public) - using contingent valuation techniques;

(ii) to evaluate whether the ESA provisions in the South Downs and Somerset Levels and Moors provide good value for money, by comparing the exchequer costs of these subsidies with the monetary valuation of the benefits.

4.31 Annual financial payments to farmers amount to £2.2 million in the South Downs and £2.5 million in the Somerset Levels and Moors. The cost to the UK public exchequer is lower than these financial payments after net receipts from the EC under the CAP are removed. Further reductions in agricultural subsidies will occur as a consequence of changes in agricultural output resulting from the ESA prescriptions. The study estimates that the net cost to the public exchequer of the ESA scheme in the South Downs (at about £1 million) is only half that estimated for the Somerset Levels and Moors (at £1.9 million).

4.32 The contingent valuation study revealed that the annual value of the benefits from the ESAs was about £80 million for the South Downs and some £53 million for the Somerset Levels and Moors. The proportion of these benefits accounted for by users - visitors and residents - was much higher for the South Downs (61%) than for the Somerset Levels and Moors (20%).

4.33 The study concluded that public expenditure on the South Downs and Somerset Levels and Moors ESAs was extremely good value for money. Benefit-cost ratios for residents and visitors are 22.5 to 1 for the South Downs, and 4.2 to 1 for the Somerset Levels and Moors; while non-user ratios are 14.4 to 1 and 16.5 to 1 respectively.

Landfill and incineration

4.34   A study carried out for the Department of the Environment by the Centre for Social and Economic Research on the Global Environment (CSERGE) and Warren Springs Laboratory set out to identify and, where possible, to value the external costs and benefits of the two main disposal to landfill routes for controlled waste in the UK - landfill and incineration - to inform consideration of a landfill levy.[1]

4.35   The study distinguishes between two categories of externality. First, there are disamenity effects such as noise, unsightliness, odour, litter and health risks. These tend to be associated more with the existence of a site or plant than with the throughput of waste. A number of studies, mainly from the USA, are reviewed. These are based on contingent valuation and hedonic pricing methods. American results suggest a willingness to pay to avoid being located near a landfill site of around £160 per household per year. The study concludes that research of this kind should be conducted in the UK for both landfill and incineration.

4.36   The second category of externality covers environmental impacts which vary according to the level of waste disposal. They include: the global warming effects of methane and carbon dioxide emissions; local air pollution; water leachate; increased volume of traffic; and pollution displacement effects of energy recovery. Using a dose-response model, it was possible to estimate a range of monetary values for most of these elements. This was done by examining the composition of a "typical" tonne of waste going to landfill and to incineration; measuring the physical impacts that each disposal route has on the relevant tonne of waste (for example the level of methane emissions); applying economic valuations to each of these impacts; and summing the results so as to produce a net external cost estimate per tonne of waste.

4.37   The main findings of the study were as follows:

(i)   the most significant external cost for landfill results from methane emissions;

(ii)   for incineration, the external costs, in particular from carbon dioxide emissions, are more than outweighed by the external benefits attributable to energy recovery;

(iii) for landfill, the estimated net external costs excluding disamenity amount to £3 to £4 a tonne for sites without energy recovery and £1 to £2 a tonne for sites with energy recovery;

---

[1] CSERGE, Warren Spring Laboratory and EFTEC (1993), *Externalities from Landfill and Incineration*, Report to the Department of the Environment.

(iv) for incineration there is an estimated net benefit excluding disamenity of about £4 per tonne of waste.

Health and environment: radon

4.38   Radon is a naturally occurring radioactive gas and is the biggest single contributor to radiation exposure in the United Kingdom. It is present in all parts of the UK, but in most areas the levels are quite low. Some of the highest levels have been found in south west England, but levels are also well above the average in parts of the Pennines and in Scotland. High indoor radon levels usually arise from radon in the soil. The National Radiological Protection Board define an "action level" at 200 becquerels per cubic metre for existing dwellings, with a lower level for new dwellings. It is estimated that radon levels in about 100,000 houses in the UK are high enough to merit action. There are a number of techniques which can be used to proof buildings against radon.

4.39   In response to the report of House of Commons Environment Select Committee on Indoor Pollution[1], the Department of the Environment commissioned the Department of Public Health and Policy at the London School of Hygiene and Tropical Medicine to carry out a study of the costs and benefits of radon proofing.[2]

4.40   The economic issue addressed in this research was whether and how far the benefits arising from reductions in the risk to human health - radon is a significant contributory cause of lung cancer particularly for smokers - were sufficient to justify the costs in terms of testing and mitigation measures.

4.41   Using estimates of the cost for each year of life gained, the study concluded that, on present evidence, measures to reduce radon levels in buildings could be cost-effective in comparison with other government funded life-extending interventions. Simple measures to reduce radon levels (such as sealing or underfloor ventilation) would be justified even for radon concentrations below the current action level. More expensive remedial work could be justified where the quantities of radon exceed the action level.

---

[1] Environment Committee, *Indoor Pollution, Sixth Report*, Vol 11, House of Commons, Session 1990-91.

[2] K Field, B Shoderu and C Normand (1993), *Cost Effectiveness of Measures to Reduce Radon in Existing Dwellings*,Report for the Department of the Environment.

References

D W Pearce and C Bann (1992), *Social Costs of Fuel Cycles*, HMSO.

CSERGE, Warren Spring Laboratory and EFTEC (1993), *Externalities from Landfill and Incineration*, Report to the Department of the Environment.

Environment Committee, *Indoor Pollution,* Sixth Report, Vol 11, House of Commons, Session 1990-91.

Environmental Resources Limited (1993), *The Valuation of Biodiversity in UK Forests*, Report for the Forestry Commission.

Forestry Commission (1993), *The Costs and Benefits of Planting Three Community Forests: Forest of Mercia, Thames Chase and Great North Forest*, Forestry Commission.

K Field, B Shoderu and C Normand (1993), *Cost Effectiveness of Measures to Reduce Radon in Existing Dwellings*, Report for the Department of the Environment.

N Hanley in association with ECOTEC Ltd, *The Valuation of Environmental Effects, Stages I and II*. Final reports published by the Scottish Office Industry Department/ Scottish Enterprise as *ESU Research Papers No.22* (1990) and *No.27* (1992).

Report by a Panel of Consultants (1993), *Stated Preference Scoping Study,* Report for Scottish Enterprise.

K G Willis, G D Garrod and C M Saunders (1993), *Valuation of the South Downs Levels and Moors Environmentally Sensitive Area Landscapes by the General Public*, Report for the Ministry of Agriculture, Fisheries and Food.

Chapter 5: Economic Instruments

Introduction

5.1   The recent report by the Department of the Environment "Making Markets Work for the Environment" describes the potential application of economic instruments to environmental policy. The advantages of economic instruments are described in that publication. This chapter summarises a number of the research reports on the subject.

5.2   Compared to regulatory measures, economic instruments will normally achieve a given level of pollution reduction at a lower cost. A financial incentive provides polluters with the flexibility to make efficient choices in the light of their own set of priorities and marginal costs of adjustment, as well as the prices faced in the market place. This is particularly important where the cost of abatement varies greatly between polluters. Decentralisation of the decision making process ensures that a given target will be met at minimum net cost.

5.3   What is perhaps less well recognised is that economic instruments can also help to overcome the problem of environmental externalities by attaching a price to using the environment. The value of environmental assets used is then allowed for in the production process in the same way as other input costs; producers are given a choice between investing in pollution abatement or paying to pollute the environment.

5.4   Environmental appraisal studies of the use of economic instruments are therefore concerned not only with how economic instruments might be used to achieve pre-determined environmental targets or quality objectives, but also with helping to define and refine precisely what those targets and quality objectives might most sensibly be and how economic instruments can be used to that end.

Water quality

5.5   In 1992, the Department of the Environment commissioned Environmental Resources Ltd and Oxford Economic Research

Associates (OXERA) to carry out a study[1] on the use of economic instruments to meet (or improve) water quality standards. The study also examined the interaction of market-based pollution charges with economic regulation of the water industry.

5.6   Various types of market instruments - emission charges, product charges, deposit refunds and marketable permits - were explored. With regard to water pollution, the deposit refund scheme was not applicable. Tradeable permits were considered inappropriate for the UK, where water quality objectives are very location-specific and there would tend to be only a small number of traders in the market.

5.7   The consultants concluded that emission charges, where the pollution is priced directly, were most relevant to the management of water resources. This involved a formula which weighted the sum of the charge on the volume of water abstracted and charges on the volume of each pollutant discharged according to the desired quality of the river. The emission charges would reflect the damage caused by the individual polluting discharges or by the abstraction of water. It was recognised, however, that a problem would be caused by diffuse pollutants such as fertilisers which are hard to monitor at the point of emission. In these cases product charges were recommended.

Air quality

5.8   The Department of the Environment commissioned London Economics in 1992 to carry out an analysis of the potential role of market mechanisms in the control of acid rain.[2]

5.9   The purpose of the study was to consider whether and in what circumstances market mechanisms could assist in the implementation of policies to abate sulphur emissions which cause acid rain. The study took as a starting point the national plan for reducing emissions of sulphur dioxide.

5.10   The approach adopted was a simulation experiment using a model of the England and Wales electricity system. (Scotland was subject to a separate study.) An inventory of other large polluting sources was made available by Warren Spring Laboratory. Attention was paid to the critical loads approach which assumes that there are threshold levels of acid deposition which the local environment can tolerate. Two possibilities were thus explored in the study: the first, reducing aggregate sulphur dioxide across the board in a manner akin to that in the national plan, had the attraction of being simpler to devise

---

[1] Environmental Resources Ltd in association with OXERA (1992), *The Use of Market Mechanisms for Water Environment*, Report for the Department of the Environment.

[2] London Economics (1992), *The Potential Role of Market Mechanisms in the Control of Acid Rain*, HMSO.

and administer; the second, focused specifically on reducing deposition at locations where critical loads were exceeded.

5.11   The conclusions were:

(i) 'market mechanisms are intrinsically more efficient economically than administrative controls in that they allow the effective balancing of the marginal costs of abatement across all the diverse sources of pollution. Permits were preferred to emission charges in that the former provided the certainty of reducing total emissions to comply with international obligations. It was suggested that permits should be issued annually to comply with international obligations, and an auctioning system could be introduced gradually which would offset the potential for participants to corner the market.

(ii) a single national bubble could save approximately £60 to £80 million annually, 16% of the total cost of abatement;

(iii) it may be possible to deliver efficiently the EC Directive targets using a weighted system of emission permits. The weighting would correspond to the damage caused by the source to which the permit applied.

5.12   The published London Economics report incorporated some separate work commissioned by the Scottish Office on the electricity supply industry in Scotland. While the policy analysis in the report was drawn at a UK level, the detailed modelling was undertaken for England and Wales only. The Scottish work was a supplementary modelling exercise. Its conclusions made for a useful addition to the original work. One conclusion, relevant to policy appraisal, was that the costs of implementing abatement targets will differ from company to company and from area to area, a feature which increases the efficiency of a tradeable permits system compared to regulation. The Department of the Environment, responding to the findings of the London Economics Report, is thus preparing a consultation paper to be launched in the autumn, on a proposed "quota-switching" scheme which is to be designed with the views of industry being taken into account, as well as drawing on similar schemes already in operation, for example, the RECLAIM[1] scheme in California.

Climate change

5.13   The Framework Convention on Climate Change requires signatory countries to take steps aimed at returning greenhouse gas

---

[1] South Coast Air Quality Management District (1993), *RECLAIM Program Summary and Rules, A Market Incentive Air Pollution Reduction Program for Nitrogen Oxides (NOx) and Sulfer Oxides (SOx)*.

emissions to 1990 levels by 2000. To meet this commitment, the UK Government has developed a programme of measures which aims to reduce economy-wide CO_2 emissions by around 10 million tonnes of carbon (mtC) in 2000, against current projections.

a) Costs of policy options and international competitiveness

5.14   The main objectives of a study[1] of the impacts of greenhouse gas control strategies which was carried out for the Department of Trade and Industry by John Pezzey at the University of Bristol, were as follows:

(i)   to assess the nature and significance of the direct and indirect implications for UK competitiveness of CO_2 emission control strategies; and

(ii) to establish a methodological framework for comparative empirical analyses of alternative CO_2 emissions control strategies.

5.15   The study consisted of three elements: the provision of a conceptual and methodological framework of the issues; a review of existing studies and models of the effects of CO_2 control on industrial competitiveness; and the provision of simple empirical illustrations of topics shown to be of interest in the framework, but not yet covered in the literature.

5.16   Two major international scenarios for CO_2 control are analysed in this report. They are:

(i)   policy action in all OECD countries to meet comparable CO_2 targets; and

(ii) policy action in the EC alone to meet comparable CO_2 targets, using uniform or non-uniform policy instruments. (The study focuses on energy and carbon taxes as the instruments of CO_2 control).

5.17   Among other things, Pezzey provides a preliminary indication of how a pure carbon tax and a pure energy tax would alter relative international costs of production for ten manufacturing sectors in seven OECD countries (the UK, USA, Japan, Germany, France, Italy and Spain).

5.18   Simple cost comparisons suggest that the effects on competitiveness of a carbon or energy tax will be greatest in the fuel

---

[1] J Pezzey (1991), *Impacts of Greenhouse Gas Control Strategies on UK Competitiveness*, HMSO.

industries themselves; that four energy-intensive sectors - iron and steel, chemicals, non-ferrous metals, and non-metallic minerals - will be affected very differently from other sectors; and that the UK is about average in its sensitivity to CO_2 control. Differences between carbon and energy taxes are significant mainly for countries using large amounts of nuclear fuel, such as Japan and France.

b) Long term strategy on road fuel duties

5.19　Increasing road fuel duty is the most cost-effective measure that might be applied in the transport sector. The choice of how to make carbon savings remains with the road user and vehicle manufacturer. The motorist will have a wide range of options including: driving more carefully and slowly; choice of new technology or smaller vehicles at point of vehicle replacement; better vehicle maintenance; combining of trip purposes; abandonment of some trips or switch to another mode; and changes in land use patterns.

5.20　The effects of fuel duty increases on road fuel demand, and hence CO_2 emissions from road transport, have been estimated by the Department of Transport using an econometric model. The core of this is an equation that uses past evidence to explain how demand for road fuel varies as fuel prices and incomes vary. This is used to predict future levels of fuel demand, given assumptions about prices and incomes, based on the fuel duty strategy.

5.21　In the November 1993 Budget Statement, the Chancellor announced that road fuel duties were to be increased by 3p per litre (including consequential VAT), and by at least 5% in real terms in successive Budgets. This strategy is expected to reduce road transport CO_2 emissions by around 2.5 mtC in 2000. Adherence to the minimum Budget commitments until 1999 should increase real fuel prices by 2000 by about 30% above the level expected without the strategy. For illustration, Figures 1 and 2 assume that the strategy continues until the 1999 Budget. Figure 1 shows that road fuel prices are expected to reach their highest real level of the last forty years. Figure 2 shows estimated CO_2 emissions from 1990 to 2000 in the base case, and with the strategy.

FIGURE 1

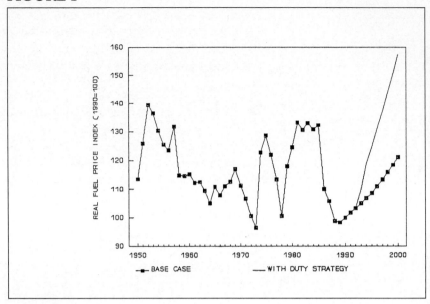

FIGURE 2

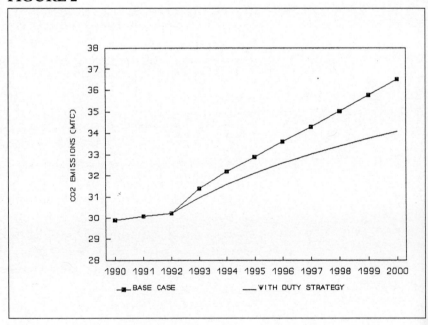

5.22   In summary, the 2.5mtC saving was derived as follows:

		mtC
- 1990 road transport CO_2 emissions	=	29.9
- base case forecast for 2000	=	36.5
- forecast for 2000 with duty increase	=	34.0
CO_2 saving in 2000	=	2.5

5.23   One of the benefits of using fuel pricing as a policy tool is the flexibility that it offers. As the target date approaches, prices can be varied to bring emissions as close as possible to the target level.

c) Tradeable credits to improve new car fuel economy

5.24   The Department of Transport has also examined a market oriented type of regulation in the form of a "tradeable credits" system. This system has been designed to reduce carbon dioxide per kilometre from passenger cars by encouraging the development and purchase of more fuel economic cars.

5.25   The proposal would not involve the allocation of "permits" to pollute, as conventionally associated with systems of "tradeable permits". The latter involve problems in deciding how to allocate permits before trading commences, and in dealing with new entrants. In contrast, the tradeable credits system described in this study[1],[2] would not require such discretionary judgements about how the system is to be started, nor would it offer any impediments to new entrants to the market. A single target level of CO_2 per kilometre would be set; new cars with lower emissions would earn credits; and new cars with higher emissions would need to obtain credits to cover the deficit between actual and target emissions.

5.26   The study examined five main policy options for achieving significant reductions in CO_2 emissions from passenger cars: fuel tax; differential vehicle tax; voluntary agreements with manufacturers; regulation of CO_2 per kilometre; and tradeable credits.

5.27   The options were evaluated with respect to the following criteria: cost-effectiveness; flexibility; ability to influence demand (directly or indirectly); ability to offer an incentive for technical improvements; ability to avoid distortions in trade and competition; ability to avoid bureaucracy; tightness of emissions control offered.

5.28   The advantages of tradeable credits are that they would:

(i)   be the least costly form of regulation. Consumers and manufacturers would be able to make choices within the overall context of a target for improvement in CO_2 emissions. Changes would be made where and when the costs were lowest;

---

[1] S R Taylor (1992), *Tradeable Credits: Variants for the Transport Sector* pp 123-137 in *Climate Change: Designing a Tradeable Permits System,* OECD Documents (1992).

[2] M St. J Fendick, S R Taylor and R R T Tinch (1993 unpublished paper), *Tradeable Credits to Reduce CO_2 Emissions from Cars.*

(ii) provide flexibility. For example, the consumer could still buy high performance luxury cars; but the need for extra credits would drive up the price, increasing incentives to cut CO_2 elsewhere in the market;

(iii) offer incentives to all manufacturers. Even the already efficient producer would still have an incentive to cut CO_2 - if the extra costs of doing so were less than the extra revenue from the sale of credits;

(iv) involve a single target. This would ensure a clear, simple signal for the consumer and the manufacturer. The single target would leave the consumer free to decide willingness to pay for, say, a powerful versus a less powerful car; and it would leave key decisions on new investment, the speed of change and the number of credits earned/required to the manufacturer;

(v) ensure that market distortions are minimised. Because the credits would be tradeable among firms, the average standard is set for the whole fleet: individual manufacturers and importers would be free to deviate from this. Thus the system does not discriminate against manufacturers which do not exhibit balanced production across the whole (size) range of the market;

(vi) leave the money involved with the buying, selling, lending and borrowing of credits largely within the motor industry. These funds could be used for investment in further technological advances.

5.29   Under the tradeable credits proposal, a single target level (or 'standard' or 'norm') of CO_2 emissions (in grammes per kilometre (g/km)) would be set. This might be 180 g/km in the first year (around the most recent average for new cars sold in the UK). The target figure would be chosen so that the need for credits to cover the less efficient vehicles in the first year would be matched approximately by the number of credits earned by the better performing vehicles. That would help to ensure a relatively easy adjustment to the new system.

5.30   The target would be tightened at a rate determined by the required reduction in emissions from cars, possibly after allowing for the expected increases in ownership and distance travelled, and trends in 'upsizing'. The target could be tightened at an annual flat rate, or by a certain annual percentage. One option would be to tighten the target more slowly to start with, then more quickly once the industry had time to adjust to the system, perhaps flattening out somewhat as the marginal costs of improvement increased. This would give an 'S'-

shaped pattern; many others may be envisaged, the final choice depending on the degree of urgency of reductions and the degree of flexibility anticipated in the industry.

5.31   Whatever the pattern of reductions in the standard, it is crucial that these are advertised several years in advance, in order that manufacturers may plan ahead, invest in research and development, and modify production plans and designs where necessary.

Waste management and recycling

5.32   A number of studies have been carried out on the potential for applying economic instruments to achieve cost-effective solutions to the waste management problem. The most general of these considered the economic efficiency, practicality and potential effectiveness of different economic instruments in achieving the environmental targets of reducing waste and encouraging recycling.[1]

5.33   Eight instruments were evaluated against the criteria of effectiveness in increasing recycling levels; ability to internalise externalities; revenue raising potential; fairness and acceptability to those involved in the waste disposal chain; and administrative feasibility. The conclusions for each of the eight are summarised in the box.

5.34   The instruments were evaluated on the basis of a cost- benefit analysis of disposal. Total costs were calculated using changes in consumer and producer surplus, where supply and demand curve slopes were determined by price elasticities. Total benefits were measured as the savings in waste collection and disposal costs. A major assumption of the analysis was that the costs of safe disposal more or less represent social costs. No attempt was made to value "intangibles" such as aesthetics, nuisance, etc.

---

[1] Environmental Resources Limited (1992), *Economic Instruments and Recovery of Resources from Waste*, HMSO.

Economic Instruments for Waste Management and Recycling

Raw materials charges: Does not reach all waste streams but, where it does, it provides the incentive to recycle. Administratively complex and thus costly. May also have adverse trade implications. Good revenue raising potential and able to internalise externalities.

Product charges: Coverage superior to raw materials but incentives to recycle at the individual firm level weak. This improves on an industry basis. Administratively complex and similar revenue raising and internalisation effects as raw materials charges.

Waste collection charges: Complete coverage and provides householders with the incentive to recycle waste. May have undesirable side effects eg fly tipping. No adverse trade implications, easy to administer, raises revenue and internalises costs.

Waste disposal charges: Complete coverage but limited incentive to recycle. The risk of fly tipping etc is also present. Good revenue raising potential. Easy to administer and successful in internalising costs.

Deposit refund schemes: Limited coverage but simple to administer and high incentive to recycle in appropriate areas. Impose net costs on society in terms of inconvenience.

Tradeable permits/targets: Good coverage and provide incentive to recycle. May be problems if the market for permits is uncompetitive. Encourages cost effectiveness. Running costs low but the set up costs are likely to be high.

Changing responsibilities: Low information requirements thus easy to administer. Effective in internalising externalities but poor revenue raising potential. Can encourage recycling and should obtain wide coverage.

Subsidies: No large incentives to recycle but reasonable coverage. Likely to be costly to administer. Not effective in internalising externalities nor in raising revenue

5.35 In a report commissioned by the Department of the Environment, Touche Ross Consultants in association with Gibb Environmental Sciences investigated the systems and mechanisms needed for the establishment of a scheme of recycling credits.[1] The object of such a scheme should be that proper compensation is paid which reflects the savings in collection and disposal costs caused by the recycling of waste.

5.36 The study considered both the short run and long run savings available to Waste Collection Authorities (WCAs) and Waste Disposal Authorities (WDAs) from each tonne of additional waste which is recycled and thus removed from the standard 'waste cycle'. Collection savings would result from lower labour and running costs, and in the long run from the need for fewer vehicles. Disposal savings would result from lower labour and running costs and, in the long run at least, from the reduced amount of space required for landfill.

5.37 This distinction between short run and long run savings is important because the value of credits must be a measure of long run savings in order to give the correct economic incentive for recycling. In the past, waste disposal credits have often been set too low. Apart from being inefficient, this has not encouraged recycling. But if credits are set too high, then there may also be excessive expenditure on the part of local authorities. The study did not consider the environmental externalities associated with landfill or incineration.

5.38 The study also concluded that recycling credits should be paid on the basis of where the savings arise. If recycling were to take place after waste had been collected and delivered to the WDA, no collection credit should be payable. If waste is incinerated before being deposited in a landfill, since this process still produces residual waste the disposal credit should be adjusted accordingly. Similarly, credits should be paid to those responsible for the saving, be it between WCAs and WDAs or to a third party.

The law of liability

5.39 As "Making Markets Work for the Environment" points out, an awareness of civil legal liability can be an important influence on the way businesses operate. To this extent, the regime of legal liability can act like an economic instrument. For instance, a consciousness of their liabilities might induce businesses to invest to reduce pollution, to pay for better monitoring, training or supervision, to put money aside for contingencies, or to take out insurance.

---

[1] Touche Ross Consultants in association with Gibb Environmental Sciences (1991), *Waste Recycling Credits: Systems and Mechanisms,* Report to the Department of the Environment.

5.40   In a paper commissioned by the Department of the Environment, Anthony Heyes focused on the economic issues relating to two models of simplified liability regimes: a strict liability regime, where polluters are responsible for all of the costs of preventing or correcting any environmental damage that they cause; and a fault-based liability regime, where polluters are responsible for any external damage only if their preventive measures have been below some minimum standard.[1]

5.41   Heyes concluded that the incentives faced by the polluter under each liability regime are identical. Preference for one type of regulatory regime would therefore stem from factors other than economic efficiency. Heyes then compared the performance of the regimes when one introduces other factors such as distributional goals, the role of insurance, and problems of implementation.

5.42   In a strict liability model, the externalities associated with pollution are fully internalised and the costs borne entirely by the polluter, whereas under a fault based regime, the costs are shared between the polluter and the consumer. The problems of assigning distributional weights, for example, on the basis of the Polluter Pays Principle, the Hicks-Kaldor criterion, and scrutiny of past government decisions and marginal tax rates for companies and households, were recognised.

5.43   The paper looked at mechanisms for spreading the risks attached to potential damage to the environment amongst polluters. In the presence of adverse selection in insurance markets due to inadequate information, low-risk firms are likely to subsidise high-risk polluters by paying excessively high premia for environmental liability insurance. Joint compensation schemes may be a superior method of spreading risk if industry participants are better informed about the environmental risks facing individual companies. Under a strict liability regime, these schemes will also have the advantage of avoiding any need for blame being attached to a particular polluter in order for remedial work to be undertaken.

5.44   Turning to problems of implementation, the paper found that polluters operating under a strict liability regime had a greater incentive to minimise the level of environmental precaution where enforcement was imperfect and in the absence of punitive damages. In contrast, under a fault-based liability regime, polluters will still continue to meet the minimum legal standards provided there is some amount of

[1] A G Heyes (1993), *The Economics of Alternative Liability Regimes as Instruments for the Control of Environmental Hazards*, Report to the Department of the Environment.

enforcement. With regard to the incentive to develop environmentally 'cleaner' technologies, this will be greater under strict liability regimes. Finally, the paper considers the incentive for defensive action by victims. With strict liability the prospect of full compensation will mean that victims have no incentive to engage in defensive action unless they are permitted to receive only a proportion of the damages if defensive action had not been carried out.

References

Environmental Resources Limited in association with OXERA (1992), *The Use of Market Mechanisms for the Water Environment,* Report for the Department of the Environment.

Environmental Resources Limited (1992), *Economic Instruments and Recovery of Resources from Waste,* HMSO.

M St. J Fendick, S R Taylor and R R T Tinch (1993 unpublished paper), *Tradeable Credits to Reduce CO_2 Emissions from Cars.*

A G Heyes (1993), *The Economics of Alternative Liability Regimes as Instruments for the Control of Environmental Hazards,* Report to the Department of the Environment.

London Economics (1992), *The Potential Role of Market Mechanisms in the Control of Acid Rain,* HMSO.

J Pezzey (1991), *Impacts of Greenhouse Gas Control Strategies on UK Competitiveness,* HMSO.

South Coast Air Quality Management District (1993), *RECLAIM Program Summary and Rules, A Market Incentive Air Pollution Reduction Program for Nitrogen Oxides (NOx) and Sulfer Oxides (SOx).*

S R Taylor (1992), *Tradeable Credits: Variants for the Transport Sector* pp 123-137 in *Climate Change: Designing a Tradeable Permits System,* OECD Documents (1992).

Touche Ross Consultants in Association with Gibb Environmental Sciences (1991), *Waste Recycling Credits: Systems and Mechanisms,* Report to the Department of the Environment.

Department of Transport (1993), *A System of Tradeable Permits for Cars* unpublished paper.

Glossary

Appraisal	the process of defining and examining options, and of weighting costs and benefits before a decision is made.
Avoided Cost Approach	a technique which seeks to value a non-marketed environmental good by measuring the actual expenditure on substitute goods which offset environmental hazards.
BATNEEC	'best available techniques not entailing excessive cost.'
Benefit-cost Ratio	a measure of the desirability of a project, useful for ranking projects where there are limited funds.
BPEO	Best Practicable Environmental Option. The option which provides the most benefit or least damage to the environment as a whole, at an acceptable cost.
Biodiversity	a term which embraces the whole of 'life on earth'. It incorporates the idea of distinctiveness at every level of life, from molecules to cells, to individuals, to species, to assemblage of species, and to ecosystems. Biodiversity may be described in terms of genes, species and ecosystems.

Bubbles	a bubble allows a firm to sum the emission limits from individual sources of a pollutant and to adjust the level of control applied to different sources as long as the aggregate limit is not exceeded.
Command-and-control Regulation	the enforcement of environmental standards through the setting of standards which must then be adhered to.
Compliance Cost Assessment	an assessment of the likely cost to businesses of complying with a new or amended regulation. The aim of policy is to minimise the burden of regulatory costs on businesses.
Congestion Charging	a charge on road use which varies according to the extent of traffic congestion.
Consumer Surplus	the excess welfare accruing to a consumer through being able to purchase some units of a good at a lower price than he or she would be willing to pay.
Contingent Ranking	a technique which assists valuation by using survey questions to elucidate orders of preferences for non-marketed goods; also known as stated preference.
Contingent Valuation	a technique which uses survey questions to estimate willingness to pay for non-marketed outputs.

Cost-benefit Analysis	a technique for calculating and weighing-up all costs and benefits relating to a particular plan, programme or project. This includes the values of those costs and benefits, some environmental, which have not or will not be reflected by actual payments.
Cost Effectiveness Analysis	the comparison of different options to find the cheapest way of meeting a predefined objective.
Discounting	the technique of converting future monetary amounts to their equivalent value in today's terms by applying a discount rate.
Dose-response Model	the relationship between the level of a pollutant and the environmental impact.
Dynamic Analysis	the study of the behaviour of an economic system when it is moving between two different equilibria.
Economic Instruments	see entry for *Market-based Instruments*.
Emissions Leakages	the degree of leakage is the amount by which emissions increase in countries which are not taking any measures, as a result of the reductions in countries which are. Emissions leakages are normally expressed as a percentage of the reductions.
Environmental Appraisal	the integration of environmental costs and benefits into a general analysis of the economic implications of proposed programmes and projects.

Environmental Accounting	the collecting of natural resource and environmental data in an accounting framework.
Environmental Assessment	a technique, often termed an Environmental Impact Assessment, for identifying the environmental effects of development projects and an important element in the procedure in land use planning for certain new developments. Procedures include the preparation of an environmental statement and appropriate public consultations prior to approval or rejection of the project.
Environmental Evaluation	the integration of environmental costs and benefits into a post-implementation review of the effectiveness of a policy or programme.
Environmental Externalities	costs or benefits which arise where economic welfare effects of an activity upon the environment are not reflected in market prices.
Environmental Statement	a document setting out the developer's own assessment of his project's likely environmental effects, which he prepares and submits in conjunction with his application for consent.
Evaluation	the ex-post examination of the effects of a policy.

Existence Value	values placed on environmental assets which are independent of their use by human beings, related instead to people's satisfaction in knowing that the object exists.
Externality Adders	the external costs and benefits which must be added to a financial appraisal in order to undertake cost-benefit analysis.
Fault-based Liability Regime	a legal system where polluters are responsible for environmental damage only if it is shown that their preventive measures were below a predetermined standard.
Financial Appraisal	an analysis confined to the cash flow implications of alternative options.
Free Riders	individuals who are able to receive the benefit from a collectively-provided good without making any payment. The light from street lighting is often cited as an example.
Hedonic Pricing	a valuation technique which estimates the value of non-marketed environmental resources from observed variations in the prices of marketed goods, such as property prices in different areas.
Hicks-Kaldor Criterion	a criterion for judging whether economic welfare is improved which concludes that proposed State B is to be preferred to existing state A if the gainers can compensate those who lose, and still be better off than before. This is regardless of whether compensation is actually paid.

Imperfect Competition	a market structure where the conditions for perfect competition are not met.
Integrated Pollution Control	an approach to pollution control in the UK which recognises the need to look at the environment as a whole so that solutions to particular pollution problems take account of potential effects upon all environmental media.
Macroeconomic Model	the study of the behaviour of the economy as a whole.
Market-based Instruments	policy instruments that achieve environmental objectives by means of incentives (i.e. charges or subsidies) to producers to lower their level of pollution.
Microeconomic Model	the study of the behaviour of individual units in an economy, notably firms, consumers and particular markets.
Monetary Valuation	the quantification of non-marketed costs and benefits, including environmental externalities, in money terms.
Natural Capital	wealth which exists in the form of environmental resources, as distinct from man-made capital.
Net Present Value	a measure of the difference between the present values of costs and benefits.
Non-user Benefits	a measure of the benefits that people receive from a resource through knowledge of its existence.

Normal Profits	that profit which is just sufficient to induce the owner-manager of a firm to remain in his present activity.
Offsets	the procedure whereby new emissions of a pollutant are 'offset' by reducing emissions from existing sources.
Option Appraisal	a term used to describe the appraisal of alternative options designed to achieve a particular objective.
Pareto Criterion	a criterion for judging whether economic welfare has increased: it is possible to change the existing resource allocation in such a way that someone is made better off and no one is made worse off.
Perfect Competition	a type of market structure where a number of conditions hold, including the presence of normal profits and identical firms who have no individual discretion over the price charged for a particular good.
Polluter Pays Principle	the idea that the cost of measures needed to improve a polluted environment to an acceptable state should be reflected in the cost of goods and services which cause pollution in production and/or consumption.
Portfolio Analysis	an approach to the management of financial assets which seeks to reflect the optimum balance between risk and return for the investor.

Potential Pareto Criterion	see entry for *Hicks-Kaldor Criterion*.
Precautionary Principle	requires that where there are significant risks of damage to the environment, precautionary action to limit the use of potentially dangerous materials or the spread of potentially dangerous pollutants is taken, even where scientific knowledge is not conclusive, if the balance of likely costs and benefits justifies it.
Present Value	the discounted value of a stream of future costs or benefits.
Price Elasticity of Demand	the percentage change in demand for a good that occurs in response to a percentage change in the price of that good.
Price Elasticity of Supply	the percentage change in supply of a good that occurs in response to a percentage change in the price of that good.
Producer Surplus	the excess welfare accruing to the owner of a factor of production through receiving a higher price for some units of a good than he or she would be prepared to sell at.
Risk Assessment	risk assessment describes the entire process by which information obtained through hazard identification, dose-response assessment, and exposure assessment is used to complete a risk characterisation.

Risk-benefit Analysis	cost-benefit analysis of options involving changes in risk to human health and environmental assets.
Scoping Studies	studies which investigate the applicability of alternative valuation techniques to different projects.
Sensitivity Analysis	analysis of the effects on the ranking of options in an appraisal of varying the projected values of certain variables.
Social Costs	costs of some activity or output which are borne by society as a whole, and which may differ from the costs borne by the individual or firm carrying out that activity or producing that output.
Stated Preference Technique	see entry for *Contingent Ranking*.
Static Analysis	the comparison of different states of an economic system when its variables are in equilibrium.
Strict Liability Regime	a legal system where polluters are responsible for all the costs of preventing or correcting any environmental damage.
Sustainable Development	development that meets the needs of the present without compromising the ability of future generations to meet their own needs.

Travel Cost Method	a valuation technique which looks at the cost of time spent travelling as a proxy for the benefit of a non-marketed environmental resource. It can be used for quantifying both environmental "goods" such as sites of scenic beauty and "bads" such as congestion.
User Benefits	benefits deriving from actual use of an environmental resource.

Printed in the United Kingdom for HMSO.
Dd. 0297796 6/94 C19 9385 9625